Gift Aid item
20 10018299 3728

AF593610

Bus Stop

an anthology of buses

compiled and designed by GAVIN BOOTH

LONDON

IAN ALLAN

First Published 1969

Published in the United Kingdom by Ian Allan Ltd, Shepperton, Surrey, and printed by the Press at Coombelands Ltd, Addlestone, Surrey

Contents

Introduction

It is difficult to pin down the reason why buses are fascinating. Tramcars and steam locomotives have, perhaps, more obvious character, yet there is an ever-growing band of bus enthusiasts who would disagree. To most people the bus is so much a part of the everyday scene that its presence is largely taken for granted—except when their bus is late. Similarly, for the gentlemen of the press, buses are only good copy when they crash or when their crews go on strike.

Still, for many the fascination is there, and it takes different forms. There are those whose interest is in the vehicles, others who concentrate on the routes; some who collect tickets, others who collect numbers; some collect photos of buses, others collect actual buses, and preserve them.

This anthology, a sort of "omnibus omnibus", is for all these people, from the youngest bus enthusiast to the oldest transport executive. It is largely a personal choice from articles, photographs and cartoons that I have enjoyed, though since these are augmented by specially commissioned articles from several leading transport writers, it is not an anthology in the strictest sense of the word. You may detect a slight Scottish bias, for which I, as a Scot, am responsible—but then there is also a slight London bias which, in a book like this, appears to be almost inevitable: when most non-transport authors write about buses, they write about London buses.

Unlike the tramcar or the steam locomotive, the bus is still very much with us in Britain. Perhaps this book will help pin down some of the reasons why buses are fascinating.

GAVIN BOOTH

Edinburgh,
October 1968

To set the scene, several well-known writers were asked to cover specific stages in the development of the motor bus, and in the development of the bus industry as we know it today.

The years to 1918: Laying the Foundations

Chas. S. Dunbar, M Inst T

Union Jack was the fleetname used by one of the larger London independent operators, the London Road Car Company Ltd. This Straker-Squire was photographed in 1906, two years before the firm amalgamated with the London General company.

[London Transport

It is a strange fact that this century opened without a single motorbus in service in London or, indeed in any other city in the world. There had been experiments in plenty but even when these seemed promising the political atmosphere of the 19th century had been against the bus engineer.

As the Industrial Revolution started in Britain when the full value of steam-power came to be realized, it was natural that British engineers should turn their attention to the possibility of moving vehicles by steam and, indeed, steam-driven locomotives were tried on roads before they were tried on rails.

By 1831 a satisfactory boiler had been

evolved and in that year Sir Charles Dance began operating a regular service four times a day between Gloucester and Cheltenham using a vehicle designed by Sir Goldsworthy Gurney. This was similar in design to the mail coach of the day with the engine and boiler at the rear and the horses replaced by a forecarriage with tiller steering, so that the vehicle was, in fact, articulated, with the front part of the coach resting on the second axle of the forecarriage.

In the same year Walter Hancock of Stratford, Essex, who had been experimenting for some years, launched a service between Stratford and London, using at first a 10-seater called "Infant". This was followed two years later by "Enterprise" which Hancock built for the London and Paddington Steam Carriage Co. It went into service on April 22nd, 1833 along the New Road (now City Road, Euston Road, etc.). Although "Enterprise" was withdrawn after only 16 days operation, Hancock put other steamers to work between Paddington and the Bank, his last bus being the 22-seater Automaton, capable of running at 20 mph.

Many readers will be familiar with the painting of a coach on the London-Birmingham road the most notable feature of which is the broad and heavy front-wheel, reminiscent of a steam-roller. This was the vehicle designed by Dr. W. H. Church of Birmingham, but it failed at a public trial in 1835 and never went into service.

In 1834 Scott Russell put six steam coaches to work between Paisley and Glasgow and these gave a reliable and successful service for four months. They would undoubtedly have continued had not a boiler explosion killed five people and badly injured others. The service was then stopped by the Court of Session and Scott Russell moved to London.

There was no technical reason why, from these beginnings, steam services should not have spread all over the country, as rapid progress had been made in a few years and the early defects of the type, notably lack of power on hills, inflexibility in control and poor steering had been largely overcome. Yet production ceased by about 1840 and before 1850 all services had stopped. The main reason was the hostility of the road authorities—usually then turnpike trusts—which levied tolls four or five times those charged for horse-drawn coaches. While these charges may often have been based on a fear of excessive road wear and by the natural hostility of those whose livelihood came from horse transport, it is a reasonable guess that much of the bias against mechanical road transport was inspired by the promoters of the rapidly-growing railways.

The practicability of steam bus services appeared to be finally killed by the Locomotive Act, 1861, and the Locomotives Act, 1865. The former limited speed to 10 mph in the country and 5 in towns while the 1865 Act reduced these limits to 4 and 2 with the additional requirement that a man with a red flag had to walk in front of every vehicle.

Despite this handicap determined inventors persisted and double-deck steam buses were run in Edinburgh in 1871 and 1872. It is not known precisely why they were withdrawn.

It was about this period that steam came into prominence as a motive power for trams. From a start between New York and Harlem in 1832, horse-drawn tramways had been introduced for town transport in every continent. The reduction in rolling resistance produced by a steel wheel on a steel rail compared with an iron-shod wheel on the roads of the day enabled a much greater number of passengers to be carried by the same horse-power at a greater speed and so offered considerable advantages. Having once put passenger street vehicles on rails it was natural to apply the same motive power as had proved so successful on the reserved tracks of the railways.

Before steam trams became universal however, the practicability of electric traction was proved. This offered such tremendous advantages in acceleration, cleanliness and ease of maintenance that few steam trams were built anywhere after the 1890s.

The relatively short-lived interest in steam trams did not deter some inventors who still thought of steam as a motive power for railless road vehicles and their efforts were helped by the "emancipation" Act of 1896 which abolished the requirement for a man to walk in front and raised permitted speeds to 14 mph for vehicles not exceeding three tons unladen, an advantage which was partly offset by the Local Government Board using its power to reduce the maximum to 12 mph.

Chas E. Lee has traced steam buses by

LEFT: Typical of urban transport for many years, an Edinburgh and District horse bus, brought out of Edinburgh's Transport Museum for some period filming.
BELOW: An early motorised vehicle in the north of Scotland, an Albion A3 dog-cart of 1904.
[Gavin Booth; R. L. Grieves collection

the Liquid Fuel Engineering Co. (Lifu), which were oil-burning, at Mansfield in 1898 and Edinburgh in 1899 and also in the latter year at Dover. Three vehicles were eventually running between Dover and Deal, but the service ceased in the summer of 1901 owing to high maintenance costs.

Nothing came of the plan of the London Steam Omnibus Co. which was to have run buses designed by Sidney Straker. Two were actually built but instead of working in London went to the Potteries Electric Traction Co., where they had a very short life. Two other Straker vehicles worked quite successfully for two years (1903-5) between Stratford-on-Avon and Brailes via Shipston-on-Stour and were only withdrawn because of non-compliance with the weight and speed restrictions of the Heavy Motor Car Order, 1904.

Meanwhile the development of the electric tram prompted efforts to apply electricity to buses but all these failed because of the inadequacy of the batteries and the necessity for frequent re-charging. Later attempts were slightly more successful but the longest period any service ran was that by the London Electrobus Co. Ltd. which ran battery-driven double-deckers between Victoria and Liverpool Street from July 1907 to March 1910.

It was the invention of the internal-combustion engine using petroleum spirit which made the motorbus practicable. Among the many names of workers in this field those of Gottlieb Daimler and Karl Benz are outstanding. Early applications were to cycles, carriages and small vans but Daimler had a petrol-driven tramcar running in 1887. How Daimler's patents came to be secured for the English company bearing his name is a complicated story but the success of F. R. Simms in bringing this off led in 1900 to the production of a charabanc designed by the same Sidney Straker whom we have already met. This vehicle was noteworthy in its drive by propeller shaft through a differential to a live back-axle.

Before this, however, two small double-deck buses with 12 hp German Daimler engines were put into service between Victoria and Kennington via Westminster Bridge on October 9th 1899. The operator was the Motor Traction Co. Ltd., which was, in fact, the London Steam Omnibus Co. renamed. The service, after being diverted to Oxford Circus instead of Victoria, was withdrawn at the end of 1900.

The London Steam Omnibus Co. was a creation of Henry John Lawson who was also connected with F. R. Simms in the formation of the (British) Daimler Motor Co. Ltd. It was Lawson who designed the first full-sized bus to run on rubber tyres (solid, of course), this vehicle running between Lewisham and Eltham in 1902-4.

While full-sized motor-buses were slow to appear, there were many instances all over the country of services being started with motor wagonettes. None of these ventures lasted long because of the high cost of maintenance, particularly on tyres, but one experiment brought a famous character to the fore in the person of Walter Flexman French, whose name is indissolubly linked with the creation of the East Kent and Maidstone and District companies. From the wagonette came the enclosed single-decker of which a number ran in London from 1902 to 1906, these including steamers run experimentally in 1904/1905 by the London Road Car Co. (two vehicles) and the London General.

April 12th, 1903 is an important date in bus history for, on that day, Eastbourne Corporation started the first municipal motor-bus undertaking in Britain (and, probably, in the world), and at the same time killed the idea of trams in the town. The vehicles used were Milnes-Daimler single-deckers, built in England by arrangement between Daimler and G. F. Milnes & Co., the tramcar builders.

Also built by Milnes-Daimler were the 34-seat double-deckers put into service in London by Thomas Tilling (three) and Birch Bros. (two) in 1904. The importance of the Milnes-Daimler double-decker was that it was a purpose-built urban motor-bus and not a converted horse-bus, although like all motorbuses until 1919, it followed horse-bus style in having a concave rocker-panel instead of straight sides.

It was another fleet of Milnes-Daimlers which really put the cat among the pigeons. The London Motor Omnibus Co. Ltd., with a famous busman, George Samuel Dicks, as traffic manager, started operations on March 27th, 1905 under the fleet name Vanguard and quickly caused the two major companies, the London General and the London Road Car Co., to push on with conversion. It was Dicks who introduced service numbers and first popularized the idea of a prominent fleet name.

The pace now quickened tremendously. At the end of 1904 there were only 20 motorbuses at work in London. By March 1908 there were 1000. Competition was intense and led inevitably to combination. The General, Road Car and Vanguard amalgamated as from July 1st, 1908 and to these was added the Great Eastern of London in 1911.

Meanwhile steam had made a come-back. The Metropolitan Steam Omnibus Co. started using Darracq-Serpollet double-deckers in 1907. These vehicles proved very suitable for the work but the enterprise came to an abrupt end in 1912 when the manufacturers in France, who had sponsored the company, went into liquidation.

A larger undertaking which had a longer

life and became the progenitor of widespread services after the days of steam was the National Steam Car Co., which employed the most successful of all the steam-bus engines — that designed by Thomas Clarkson. As a manufacturer Clarkson provided the buses for the Torquay and District Motor Omnibus Co. Ltd., which operated successfully from 1903 to 1907. He also sold his buses to three railway companies, the GWR, the NER, and the LSWR, as well as to several London operators. When he eventually realized that his customers would buy no more, because they had decided to use petrol, he started his own operating company. The National operated in London from 1909 to 1919 and had a fleet of 184 buses at its maximum. The last steam-bus in Britain ran at Ryde in 1923.

But this is running too far ahead. When the General, greatly enlarged by the amalgamations of 1908, really pushed ahead with motorization it faced the problem of standardizing and this it solved by deciding to build its own buses. The former Vanguard overhaul works at Walthamstow were used to produce type X in 1909 and from this evolved the famous B-type, whch made its first appearance in October 1910. It was this vehicle which saved the General from possible extinction, for its position in 1910 was precarious after losses on the change of traction.

Tillings who, as already mentioned, started motor operation in 1904, were largely responsible for a successful hybrid—the petrol-electric—which used a petrol motor to generate current, this in turn being employed to move the road wheels. Being without gears the petrol-electric was easily mastered by former horse-drivers. It also had the valuable characteristic of the electric motor's high starting torque making for rapid acceleration. After experimental use from 1907 the Tilling-Stevens TTA1 became the company's standard vehicle both in London and the provinces from 1911 onwards.

The position in the provinces differed considerably from that in London during the first decade of the century and indeed until after the 1914-18 war. Almost every town of importance had a tramway system and the country districts managed very well with horse transport, either to the nearest railway station or to the local market town. Where the motorbus did offer prospects was in providing services where new railway construction might not pay.

J. M. Cummings in an Omnibus Society paper drew attention to the steam buses operated by the Belfast and Northern Counties Railway between Whiteabbey and Greenisland in 1902. In 1903 motor wagonettes were put on as feeders to the Lynton and Barnstaple, but, after only a month, these were sold to the Great Western Railway which used them between Helston and the Lizard. The North Eastern Railway started two services in the East Riding, also in 1903, and the Great North of Scotland began the 17 mile run between Ballater and Braemar in 1904. In the same year the London and South Western began an Exeter-Chagford service.

Other early rural services were those of the Sussex Motor Road Car Co. Ltd., between Worthing and Pulborough (1905), the Headcorn, Sutton Valence and Maidstone Motor Omnibus Co. Ltd. (1904) and the Vale of Llangollen Engineering, Bus and Garage Co. Ltd. (1905). The Sussex Co. was the progenitor of Southdown Motor Services.

The British Electric Traction group formed, in 1904, the Birmingham and Midland Motor Omnibus Co. Ltd., but this venture was initially a failure. In 1907 the company reverted to horse traction but the vehicles were sent to Deal where they were so successful as to become the foundation of the present East Kent Road Car Co. When the BMMO restarted with motors in 1912 it did so with petrol-electrics but, like the London General, it finally secured its position by building its own buses, the well-known and remarkable SOS. Other BET companies developed bus sections, which expanded well beyond the tramway areas. So, too, did other tramway undertakings, notably the Bristol Tramways and Carriage Co., which also developed an important manufacturing side.

Similarly, the Scottish Motor Traction Co., although successful from its start in 1906, really got going after it started in 1912 to build the Lothian, the most notable feature of which was the driver's position beside the engine.

One of the few important industrial towns which never had trams was Widnes. This small municipal undertaking is worth remembering for its successful operation of the first double-deckers with enclosed tops. Four Commers were put into service in 1909 and worked with the top covers until some time after 1914 when they were taken off to accommodate coal-gas bags. Other undertakings which used coal-gas because of petrol shortage during the war included Bartons of Long Eaton (another pioneer concern) and several BET companies.

When hostilities broke out in 1914, the War Office was still horse- and rail-minded, the few mechanical vehicles the Army possessed being regarded as the toys of enthusiastic young officers. Before long, however, the value of motor transport became apparent and large numbers of vehicles were commandeered. The London General, for instance, lost altogether 1600 buses. Fortunate were the undertakings using petrol-electrics as the Army did not want them.

As the war went on increasing numbers of men learned about motors and when at the end of the struggle, thousands of vehicles had to be disposed of, there was every opportunity for newcomers to launch out into transport. The year 1918 was the last in which train and tram were dominant in British local transport.

One of the London buses that went to war in 1914. This MET Daimler, carrying wounded 'Tommies' from Antwerp, arrives at Ghent in October 1914.
[London Transport

1919-1928: Prelude to Control

John F. Parke

A traffic scene in Finsbury Park in April 1923. The driver of B2248 probes a mechanical breakdown, while a K-type passes by on the other side.

[London Transport

Although many of the participants may have been unappreciative of the fact, having seized the opportunity of entering the bus business in the somewhat favourable circumstances which presented themselves after the 1914-18 war, the period from 1919 to 1928 can well be considered as the principal formative period of the industry as it is today. It saw the development of specialised passenger chassis, the large scale use of four-wheel brakes and of pneumatic tyres for large vehicles on the mechanical side and the spread of facilities throughout the country on the operating side. The larger undertakings became increasingly imbued with a sense of true public service and, by the end of the period, the smaller concerns were comparably minded through, more often than not, the enthusiasm of their principals. These factors coupled with the success of the four main line railway companies in obtaining road transport powers in 1928 created a favourable atmosphere for the introduction of the Road Traffic Act, 1930, and the effects thereof which are indicated in the next chapter.

Wartime impressment of vehicles and the

concentration of the resources of manufacturers upon War Department requirements had led to a gradual diminution in the number of buses on the road and much of the first postwar year was spent in restoring fleet levels to at least those of 1917—the following year had seen a drop of roughly a fifth. Many of the additional vehicles were adapted from WD type chassis and the smaller ones were quite frequently war surplus units since there was a marked tendency to release these first. With a distinct advantage in speed and the added comfort associated with pneumatic tyres these light vehicles often provided serious competition for the bigger buses of the more conservative larger concerns and also for the trams. In most cases, however, the trams were owned by the local authority from which bus operators needed licences to ply for hire and care was taken to ensure some degree of protection. It seemed on the other hand to be relatively rare for the local councils to have any obvious affection for the larger concerns whether or not they were old-established and some went as far as to encourage rivalry.

The potential pattern of operation was already apparent. The British Electric Traction Co. Ltd. had already developed bus services in association with many of the tramway undertakings which it had established in various parts of the country and had also initiated operations in other areas through the British Automobile Traction Co. Ltd. These went back to the preceding decade but direct operation was, as it transpired, to be short lived with responsibility being transferred to subsidiary companies save for the London buses which continued until their transference to the London Passenger Transport Board. The pattern of subsidiaries had already been established with the establishment of the East Kent, Maidstone & District and Southdown companies and the first and third of these significantly embodied in addition a Thomas Tilling interest. There was a similar common interest in Bournemouth & District Motor Services Ltd. which became Hants & Dorset in 1920 and a member of all four boards —chairman of three—was Walter Flexman French, who was also managing director of the United Service Transport Co. Ltd.,

An Edinburgh Corporation football match special of the 1920s. 153(SG1300) was a 1920 normal-control Leyland with 32-seat Cowieson body. [*Leyland*

which was one of the earlier developers of seasonal coach services from London to the seaside.

Initially Thomas Tilling, lacking the tramway interests of BET, had more spadework to do if it was to establish itself in areas other than London and Brighton where it already had substantial operations. Some of the earlier essays had already been absorbed by BAT companies or were formed in 1919 like the Eastern Counties Road Car Co. Ltd. Tilling capital was increased substantially in 1920 and this was followed in due course by the acquisition of a considerable holding in BAT. It is convenient at this juncture to look ahead to a late stage in the period under review and record that in May, 1928, the BAT company was reconstructed and given the title of Tilling and British Automobile Traction Ltd. In the process the shareholdings of Thomas Tilling in provincial companies were exchanged for T & BAT shares and this was done also with a number of what had hitherto been British Electric Traction companies. This did not, however, apply to a number of the latter's interests such as Birmingham & Midland, Northern General, Potteries and South Wales.

There were in this period other groups, mostly sprung from tramway origins, which endured wholly or in part well beyond 1929. One was the National Electric Construction Co. Ltd. with City of Oxford and Mexborough and Swinton already engaged in motorbus and trolleybus operation respectively and with Rhondda Tramways, South Wales Commercial Motors (ancestor of Western Welsh) and Torquay Tramways putting buses on the road in 1920. The remaining company in this group, the Musselburgh & District Electric Light and Traction Co. Ltd., entered the bus field in February, 1928, and so joined the very few Scottish undertakings controlled by London-based companies. Meanwhile Torquay Tramways had purchased Devon General in the summer of 1922 and transferred to the reconstructed company all its own bus services thus forming the basis for present DG operations.

Another group with interests both sides of the border was that usually known as Balfour, Beatty which had already commenced bus operation in connection with its tramway concerns and was to continue this policy. In Scotland the Scottish General Omnibus Co. Ltd. was formed in 1919 to take over the bus services of the Falkirk & District Tramways started before the 1914-18 war and the Wemyss & District Tramways commenced bus services in August, 1922. Four years later it was to purchase control of the General Motor Carrying Co. Ltd. and Scottish Utility Motors Ltd. and strengthen further the hold of the group on the Kingdom of Fife and areas north and west thereof. Indeed when the Scottish Motor Traction Co. Ltd. bought the SGO group on behalf of its subsidiary W. Alexander & Sons Ltd. early in 1930 there were no fewer than 11 concerns to be transferred. South of the border the Balfour, Beatty interests were concentrated largely in a broad band across the Midlands which was

A full-fronted 1927 Albion with Croall body being overhauled at the Edinburgh works of the Scottish Motor Traction company. [*Scottish Omnibuses*

hardly surprising in view of the association with the Midland Counties Electric Supply Co. Ltd. The larger concerns were the Midland General Omnibus Co. Ltd. registered in 1920 and Mansfield District Traction which had resumed bus operation in 1919 affer a wartime break. Notts and Derby was not to seek powers for conversion to trolleybuses and for bus operation until 1928, the year which saw the first operation by the Leamington & Warwick and an announcement that Cheltenham District was to seek bus powers.

A smaller tramways group was Provincial Tramways which had had a number of its operations taken over by municipalities but it had started motor operations in connection with the Great Grimsby Street Tramways Company as early as 1907 and had also obtained powers for the Gosport & Fareham Tramways Company. The Imperial Tramways Co. Ltd. with directors who were also on the board of Bristol Tramways & Carriage Co. Ltd. had been operating buses in connection with the Middlesbrough, Stockton-on-Tees and Thornaby Tramways but these were purchased by the three corporations under Acts of 1919 together with the trams, and Middlesbroughal so took the opportunity in conjunction with Eston UDC to form the Teesside Railless Traction Board to acquire the North Ormesby, South Bank, Normanby and Grangetown Railless Traction Company. This concern had been financed locally.

In 1919 there were 28 municipal undertakings with motorbuses and 15 more started operations during that year in some cases by purchase but more usually by the development of feeder services to tram routes. The 43 undertakings recorded in the 1920 Motor Transport Yearbook operated 500 vehicles between them whereas the 97 in the 1928-29 volume were working 3,568 and that at a time when tramway replacement had hardly become general policy at least in the larger towns and cities. Birmingham had bought the business of the Birmingham & Midland Motor Omnibus Co. Ltd. within the city in October, 1914, and despite wartime difficulties had 52 buses at work on March 31, 1919. Ten years later the fleet had grown to 297, of which 22 were one-man operated and seated variously 23, 24 and 25 passengers. As it turned out the municipalities were to lose interest in this type of operation when it was confined in the main to vehicles not seating more than 20. Eastbourne, which could claim to be the pioneer so far as municipalities were concerned, was working 35 buses in 1919 compared with 53 in 1929 and two reasons for the relatively small increase vis-a-vis many of the other undertakings were the high state of development reached at an early stage and the marked improvement in the performance of the vehicles which enabled so much more to be done with only a small fleet increase.

The effect of improvements in bus design was indeed such that the bus miles run by 85 municipalities in the year ended March 31, 1929, amounted to more than 90,750,000 which was more than twice the figure for 1926-27. The number of undertakings had risen by 14 and the number of vehicles had increased by 90 per cent. These significant figures were moreover obtained despite the marked increase that there was in bus operation in the latter part of the twenties, but it should be pointed out that the average capacity of vehicles was tending to rise. The widespread introduction of forward-control models for both single- and double-deck operation was a major factor in this respect and in this field the London General Omnibus Company with its K and S types and then the much-improved NS had done a good deal of pioneering with the aid of AEC, its fellow member in the Underground group. This should not be taken as implying that other manufacturers were doing nothing and the emergence during the decade under review of the Leyland Lion and Dennis E and also the Tilling-Stevens B9 marking that manufacturer's serious entry into the field of gear-driven buses were definite stages in progress towards the type of single-deck bus that was, in the outcome, to persist until after the 1939-45 war. Although traffic was increasing steadily, there was not then so marked an inclination to think of long provincial routes in terms of double-deck operation and this is clearly indicated by the persistence of the two large operators which manufactured their own vehicles, Birmingham & Midland and Bristol Tramways, concerning themselves almost exclusively with single-deckers. The former did supply a number of SOSs to fellow-members of the BET group such as Northern General, Potteries, and Trent but Bristol was in the market on a much wider scale and its very successful B type, known for some time as the Superbus, figured in a number of fleets including those of some municipalities.

Of even more significance was the entry into the market of the Leyland Titan double-deck and six-cylinder Tiger single-deck chassis. The following chapter quite properly refers to them because their influence was by then even more profound, but it was none the less apparent by 1928 and it was equally clear that the advent of a fast and smooth-running double-decker was turning the thoughts of many operators towards the wider use of the type on country routes. Similarly the presence on the market of large and better suspended single-deck chassis created more interest in the possibilities of long-distance coach services. Prior to 1925 most coach operation had taken the form of seasonal services to coastal resorts from inland centres and there were also, of course, many examples of what were later to be termed excursions and tours from such resorts. On February 11, 1925, Greyhound Motors Ltd., of Bristol, initiated a regular once-daily coach service between that city and London and claimed it, with reason, to be the first daily long-distance service of over 100 miles in the country. The normal-control Dennis coaches used were fitted with cushion tyres rather than pneumatics but the latter were fitted to the ADCs which succeeded them. The great increase in the reliability of the pneumatic tyres was significant. They had for some time been fitted to the lighter types of bus and coach often of American, such as Chevrolet, Reo, Dodge and International, or European, such as Auto-Traction, Lancia, and Saurer, origin. The vehicles were fast but generally their capacity was limited and the possibility of carrying as many as 30 passengers in reasonable comfort that was provided by the new forward-control chassis made the whole prospect more attractive. For various reasons some of the larger companies still hesitated and many of the long-distance routes were pioneered by relatively small independent concerns which quite frequently competed amongst themselves. Frequently the coaches had been obtained under hire purchase agreements and the battlefields of the earlier days of long-distance express services were strewn with the corpses of businesses that could not stand the pace. However that might be, it was estimated that on the basis of returns by 1,425 operators for the year to March 31, 1929, some 3,500 out of 30,000 were coaches and the basis for the present network of coach services had been established.

Another field in which progress had been made was that of trolleybus operation although, as things have turned out, this was to be a shorter phase of passenger transport operation than was then expected. There had, of course, been earlier examples and reference has already been made to the Teesside undertaking, but the period saw the introduction of no fewer than 16 systems and the abandonment of those at Halifax and Leeds. There were 23 on which services were worked with the mileages at Wolverhampton, Bradford, Ipswich and Hastings in that order all in double figures and the smallest mileages at Southend (1.24) and York (1.25). One of these was to expand and the other to vanish.

The shadows of the imminent consolidation of the bus industry were spreading. The main line railways were negotiating with many of the large concerns and developments such as the merging under the Crosville banner of the original bearer of the title with the Llandudno Coaching & Carriage Company and Wrexham & District Transport were soon to follow. In the west country the National Omnibus & Transport Co. Ltd., which had extended its interests there and also north and east of London after disposal of its London bus business to the LGOC, had already taken in in 1927 the sizeable Devon Motor Transport and Cornwall Motor Transport businesses founded by Commander F. T. Hare, and in Scotland the Scottish Motor Traction Co. Ltd., which had already been pursuing a policy of steady expansion by purchase, was reformed in August, 1929, with railway participation and was poised for the radical reorganisation of operations which was to take place.

1929-1939: The Road Traffic Act and After

James FitzJames

The effects of the granting of Road Transport powers to the railway companies in 1928 were soon to be seen. Wisely the railways decided against entering into competition on routes already served and instead acquired interests in existing operators. This was achieved in various ways and the position in England and Wales will be examined first. Agreements were made to purchase shares in undertakings forming parts of either the British Electric Traction or the Tilling and British Automobile Traction groups, although some BET companies remained without railway participation. New companies were created by National Omnibus and Transport in which the appropriate railway company took up shares. These companies were Western National, Southern National and Eastern National; the LNE and LMS railways were both involved in the last as the Tilbury section of the LMS in Essex made it difficult to set up separate companies for the areas of each railway company. Other concerns were acquired by T & BAT and railway interests together; of these probably the largest was United Automobile Services which served an area stretching from East Anglia to across the border into Scotland. The assets of the Crosville, East Midland and Hebble companies were purchased by the railways who for a time operated the services themselves until new companies were formed in which either T & BAT or BET took up shares equal to the railways. In Yorkshire joint committees were set up with the corporations of Halifax, Huddersfield, Sheffield and Todmorden whereby railway owned services were put under common management

An SMT 1930s line-up on Cramond Bridge, near Edinburgh. In the right foreground is a 1932 AEC Regal/Alexander, followed by a 1928 normal-control Star with Short body. Behind the Star is a 1930 Leyland Tiger/Cowieson, and behind this, another AEC Regal.
[Scottish Omnibuses

with the services of the respective municipalities. National Omnibus was acquired by Thomas Tilling in 1931 but with other subsequent Tilling purchases remained outside the T & BAT group. The formation in 1931 of Eastern Counties Omnibus Co. combined the East Anglian section of United Automobile (including the body-building factory at Lowestoft) with Eastern Counties Road Car of Ipswich, Ortona of Cambridge and Peterborough Electric Traction. The LNER had interests in all four of the old operators and the LMS in the Peterborough company so that both companies obtained shares in the new company, the total of which was approximately equal to the number allotted to T & BAT. In addition United retained a substantial investment in the new company. Bristol Tramways in which GWR took an interest in 1929 was transferred to the control of Western National in 1931 and Western Transport, a T & BAT company with GWR participation, was absorbed by Crosville in 1933 as a result of which GWR obtained a share in Crosville. Apart from increases in the amounts of cash invested subsequent changes in railway investments were few. By 1939 the main subsidiaries of the three large groups with the railways interested in each were as follows:—

BET—Devon General (GWR/SR), Hebble (LMS/LNER), Mexborough & Swinton (—), Midland Red (LMS/GWR), Northern General (LNER), Oxford (GWR), Potteries (—), Rhondda (—), South Wales (—), Western Welsh (GWR), Yorkshire Woollen District (LMS/LNER).

T & BAT—Aldershot (SR), Crosville (LMS/GWR), Cumberland (LMS), Eastern Counties (LNER/LMS), East Kent (SR), East Midland (LNER/LMS), East Yorkshire (LNER), Hants & Dorset (SR), Lincolnshire (LNER/LMS), Maidstone & District (SR), North Western (LMS/LNER), Ribble (LMS), Southdown (SR), Southern Vectis (SR), Thames Valley (GWR/SR) Trent (LMS/LNER), United Automobile (LNER), West Yorkshire (LMS/LNER), Wilts & Dorset (SR), Yorkshire Traction (LMS/LNER).

TILLING—Brighton, Hove & District (—), Eastern National (LNER/LMS), Southern National (SR), United Counties (—), Westcliff (—), Western National (GWR).

Among other large operators in which there was no railway participation were the Balfour Beatty group of Llanelly & District, Mansfield District, Midland General and Notts & Derby companies, the Red & White group of Red & White Services, United Welsh, Cheltenham District (previously owned by Balfour Beatty) and a number of smaller concerns, Barton Transport of Beeston and the Lancashire United and West Riding companies.

In Scotland there was no large established group in 1929 and the two railways operating north of the border came to an arrangement with the Scottish Motor Traction Company of Edinburgh whereby a new SMT company was formed to become the basis of a group covering the greater part of Scotland, but it took until 1932 before this plan came to fruition. In the meantime the LMS railway had early in 1929 taken on its own account an interest in the new MacBrayne company formed in the previous year by Burns & Laird Lines, a member of the Coast Lines shipping group and later joined in setting up The Highland Transport Company which in 1930 took over the business of Inverness & District Motor Services; these two transactions did not come into the agreement with SMT. A feature of the arrangements which the railways made with SMT prevented their participation in the BET-owned Scottish General Transport of Kilmarnock and the T & BAT-owned Caledonian of Dumfries. SMT soon acquired W. Alexander & Sons of Falkirk which was allocated the area covering the midlands and north east of Scotland and with the subsequent merging of many undertakings, of which the largest was the Scottish General Omnibus group, was to become one of the most substantial company operators in Great Britain in terms of the number of vehicles owned. Another SMT acquisition in 1929 was Midland Bus Services of Airdrie. In Aberdeenshire the LNER was a bus operator in its own right as it had inherited the services of the Great North of Scotland railway which had been commenced as long ago as 1904; these services were handed over to the Alexander complex in 1930. The LMS had also built up bus services in Ayrshire and Renfrewshire which were operated in co-operation with Scottish General Transport. Towards the end of 1931 the BET agreed to transfer its interest in SGT along with the latter's subsidiaries to SMT and within a few months SGT absorbed other interests of SMT in south west Scotland including the greater part of Midland Bus Services; in

June 1932 the name of SGT was changed to Western SMT. The T & BAT-owned Caledonian was not included in this re-arrangement and indeed remained outside the SMT group for some considerable time afterwards. Returning to 1930 we find that the LMS railway had taken control of Glasgow General Omnibus & Motor Services and other operators in Lanarkshire. These were merged under GOC in 1932 and control transferred to SMT after which the name of GOC was changed to Central SMT in June of that year. From then on acquisitions by SMT were absorbed or managed by one of the four companies, SMT, Alexander, Western SMT and Central SMT. Among these were Lanarkshire Traction managed by Central from 1932 and Lawson managed by Alexander from 1936. The former SGT subsidiaries at Greenock and Rothesay remained as separate subsidiaries of Western SMT, indeed the tramways at Rothesay continued to operate until the end of the summer of 1936.

The position in London was that while by far the largest operator was the London General Omnibus Company, bus services were also provided by Thomas Tilling, T & BAT and a very considerable number of small operators, while tramway services were operated by the London County Council, other local authorities and also companies associated with the Underground group. Bus services outside the central London area in which LGOC had an interest were provided by associated companies most of which were merged in 1931 under the name of London General Country Services. Coach services developed by LGOC in the period up to 1930 were transferred to a separate company, Green Line Coaches, formed in that year. However in 1933 under the provisions of the London Passenger Transport Act, bus, coach and tramway services in a special area surrounding the capital were all transferred to the London Passenger Transport Board created by the Act. The LPTB also took over the Underground and Metropolitan railways and came to a working arrangement with the main line railways operating within the special area.

In some one hundred provincial cities and towns services by bus, tram and trolleybus were provided by local authorities. As time passed many tramway services were replaced by buses or trolleybuses. Some

On July 1st the following undertakings were transferred to the London Passenger Transport Board:

RAILWAYS

Metropolitan District Railway
London Electric Railway
City and South London Railway
Central London Railway
Metropolitan Railway

TRAMWAYS

London County Council, Barking, Bexley, Croydon, Dartford, East Ham, Erith, Ilford, Leyton, Walthamstow, West Ham, London United, Metropolitan Electric, South Metropolitan Electric

OMNIBUSES AND COACHES

London General, London General Country Services, Overground, Tilling & British Automobile Traction, Green Line Coaches

Notice will be given as certain other undertakings are absorbed

All inquiries should be addressed to

LONDON PASSENGER TRANSPORT BOARD

55, Broadway, Westminster, S.W.1

Telephone: VICtoria 6800
Telegrams: Passengers Sowest London

C/373/33

A poster announcing the formation of the London Passenger Transport Board in 1933.

municipal services were handed over for management or operation to bus companies in the area concerned. Examples of such arrangements included those at Dover, Bristol, Gloucester, Worcester, York, Keighley, Scarborough, Carlisle, Ayr, Kilmarnock, Kirkcaldy and Perth. The precise details differed in the various places and in some of the cases mentioned the local authority never operated the services itself.

By 1929 the pattern of long distance coach services had begun to emerge and a selection showing that many were in the hands of the smaller operators follows. Scott's Azure Blue Coaches were operating between Edinburgh and Inverness and also two-day services to London, while the overnight Edinburgh-London service was provided by Thomson's Tours. Scottish Clan Motorways ran from Glasgow to Aberdeen and Lowland Motorways from Glasgow to Manchester. A number of operators shared the Newcastle-London route and several competing services operated from Blackpool and other Lancashire towns to London. On the other hand Newcastle-Liverpool services were provided by the larger operators and Midland Red had long established services from Birmingham to Welsh and Somerset coastal towns. Black & White Motorways based on Cheltenham operated thence to London, the Midlands and South Wales with a number of other operators competing on the London-South Wales section. The Bristol-London service was in the hands of Greyhound Motors who also worked from Bristol to Devon, the Midlands and Bournemouth and between Bournemouth and London. Elliott Brothers of Bournemouth (Royal Blue Automobile Services) operated to London, the West Country, the Midlands and along the South Coast. However, a substantial share of services between Sussex and London was in the hands of Southdown. George Ewer's Grey-Green coaches provided services between London and East Anglia in addition to seasonal services to South Coast and other resorts. This list is far from exhaustive but it may be noted that with the exception of some of the Lancashire-London services and those of George Ewer almost all of those referred to had by 1939 come into the hands or under the control of companies in the large groups.

In 1929 the licensing of motor bus services was in the hands of local authorities and the relative strictness of control varied from place to place. Many of these authorities issued licence numbers or plates to be carried on approved vehicles and, to quote an example, vehicles of United Automobile Services could be seen carrying numbers allocated by a dozen or so different places. All this was changed by the passing of the Road Traffic Act, 1930, which divided the country into thirteen traffic areas each having commissioners to exercise control over all public service vehicles in their areas. Each vehicle required a certificate of fitness or a certificate of conformity to type and a road service licence was required before vehicles could be used as stage or express carriages. Vehicles could be used as contract carriages, that is for private parties, without requiring a road service licence. The thirteen traffic areas were Northern (A), Yorkshire (B), North Western (C), West Midland (D), East Midland (E), Eastern (F), South Wales (G), Western (H), Southern (J), South Eastern (K), Northern Scottish (L), Southern Scottish (M) and Metropolitan (N). Conditions in the Metropolitan traffic area differed in certain respects from those in the other areas. In 1933 adjustments were made to some of the areas after the passing of the London Passenger Transport Act and the Road & Rail Traffic Act, the most important being the disappearance of the Southern traffic area. The general principles of the 1930 Act are still in force, there having been only a number of changes in detail from time to time. Tramways and trolleybuses were affected but little by the 1930 Act, their operations continuing under existing legislation.

On the vehicle side, the new Leyland "T" range of passenger vehicles (Tiger, Titan and Titanic) had been introduced at the 1927 Commercial Motor Show but comparatively few had entered service before 1929. The Titan with "lowbridge" double-deck body introduced a feature which enabled heavily loaded rural services throughout the country to be worked by double-deckers for the first time. A new generation of passenger vehicles had arrived and it was not long before the other leading manufacturers brought out vehicles of similar up-to-date specification. The next important development was the introduction of oil engines for heavy motor vehicles and in a very short time the greater economy of this equipment made it more common in use on large vehicles than the petrol

A line-up of the first Leyland Titan TD1s supplied to Alexanders in 1929.
[The Scottish Omnibus

engine it had replaced. There was however still a market for small capacity vehicles on lightly loaded services which had been fulfilled previously by vehicles of continental and transatlantic manufacture. Among these was the Chevrolet which was assembled in Great Britain by General Motors, the English subsidiary of the American corporation of similar name. Another English subsidiary of General Motors was Vauxhall Motors of Luton and in 1931 this company produced its first British manufactured commercial vehicle and gave it the name Bedford. Since then the Bedford has retained a very large share of the market for lightweight buses and coaches. Built between 1932 and1936 another vehicle of considerable interest was the AEC Q type which with the engine placed on the offside between the axles was a departure from the established front-engined vehicle. Some 350 vehicles of this type were built of which just over 20 were double-deckers, one of these having three axles. As might be expected from the traditional builders of London's buses, more than half of the Q type were supplied to London Transport but the others could be found in various parts of Great Britain and some were exported to Australia and New Zealand. A few years later a further development manufactured specially for London Transport and known as the TF type had its engine lying on its side to the rear of the driver's cab and was, perhaps surprisingly, built by Leyland. A yet more advanced vehicle, of which only one was built, was the Leyland Panda. It was probably intended to be shown at the Commercial Motor Show of 1939 which because of the war did not take place, but it did eventually enter service in 1941 when it joined the fleet of Alexander, Falkirk with a body built by the operator. The Panda had its engine under the floor and as its length was greater than that permitted at the time for a two axle vehicle, it had three axles of which two were at the front as on a number of goods vehicles and the comparatively rare Leyland Gnu all of which however had the engine at the usual frontal position. But for the war it is likely that more Pandas would have been built but another decade was to pass before the underfloor-engined vehicle was to come into its own.

1939-1945: The Bus at War

A. Alan Townsin, MI Mech E

It is sometimes suggested that the period of the second world war was one of unrelieved gloom so far as buses were concerned, with austerity vehicles, drastically reduced services, flat grey paintwork, producer gas trailers and the black-out.

All these things played their part, but their effect was far from uniformly spread either in the geographical or the time-scale sense. In many fleets the only immediate indication of the war was the black-out. This was enforced at the outbreak of war, in September 1939, and continued until the end of hostilities in Europe.

New vehicles, often painted in normal pre-war livery, apart from the mandatory white mudguard and platform edging and generally a deliberately dull roof colour, continued to be delivered to many fleets in fair numbers for about a year. What is more, these early wartime deliveries were often superior to their pre-war predecessors,

A wartime scene in Sheffield, with London Transport ST891 helping to move the peak-hour crowds.

and in some respects reached a standard which has remained unique. Coach production, on the other hand, virtually ceased before the end of 1939. Most manufacturers shelved plans for new model announcements, but Leyland were probably too deeply committed to production of the TD7 version of the Leyland Titan to hold back. Its specification, which owed a good deal to the TD6c models which had been built specially for Birmingham Corporation, was announced in the technical press a few weeks after the outbreak of war. Many regular Titan users received at least one batch of this model with bodywork to peacetime standards before normal production ceased, and their passengers thus enjoyed what was probably the quietest ride offered in any production diesel bus.

In terms of technical development, the most outstanding buses delivered during this period were London Transport's first production batch of 150 RT-type double-deckers, with chassis made by AEC and bodywork built in London's Chiswick works. But even the run-of-the-mill 1940 bus was generally fully up to immediate pre-war standard. The company-owned bus fleets continued to receive their normal patterns of single-deckers, often varying from company to company, so that a Bristol L5G with ECW body for United Automobile Services was quite different in appearance from one meant for the Eastern Counties or North Western concerns.

But initially, Britain's lone battle for survival after the fall of France in the summer of 1940 began to alter the position. Some factories had gone over to military output at the outbreak of war—notably Bedford, whose newly-introduced OB coach or bus model was only built in small numbers before production stopped. By the winter of 1940/1941 new buses had become really scarce, and delivery virtually ceased later in 1941.

Similar remarks applied to some other supplies, notably paint, and some operators had begun to put their fleets into one form or another of wartime livery. Grey was the most common choice, but the shades used varied considerably. Other colours, if that word is justifiable, were red oxide, khaki and olive green. Most of these were unvarnished, although some operators found that they were far from durable in this form and later reverted to the use of varnish. In most cases vehicles were painted in one shade with no relieving colour, but some operators used combinations of colours and some of these were quite attractive—I personally liked Manchester Corporaton's wartime red and grey rather better than the previous red and cream. A few operators managed to keep going with their normal liveries and even managed to maintain a smart appearance.

But some deterioration was inevitable in most fleets and make-do-and-mend methods were normal. But there was wide variation in maintenance standards. Ironically, some fleets that were used to withdrawing buses after seven years' service—and this was not uncommon in 1939—were in serious trouble when they had to keep 10-year-old vehicles running. Some other concerns that had voluntarily adopted policies of rebuilding or rebodying old buses before the war—the Tilling and SMT company groups come to mind—were often much better able to cope, even though they ended the war period with some vehicles of the then-unheard-of age of 16 or 18 years still in service. Putting new bodies on old chassis became common practice in many fleets in wartime.

By the mid-war period the services operated had often been severely cut. The pressure to save fuel was considerable and 50 per cent cuts in frequency on important inter-urban stage routes were common. It was frequently impossible to board a bus on such a service, even in the mid-morning off-peak. Express services were curtailed and then stopped entirely except where communities would have been isolated. On the other hand extra services to serve war factories and military bases stretched the resources of many operators to the limit.

In some ways the introduction of substitute fuels might have been expected to help. Certain operators had, with Government encouragement, been working on producer gas plant since before the outbreak of war. A workable scheme using a small trailer was evolved and tolerable results were obtainable with it, given a degree of driving skill and luck.

But hill-climbing performance suffered greatly and breakdowns were frequent. Operators were expected to convert ten per cent of their fleets to work on gas but many either did not achieve this figure or avoided using the converted vehicles as much as possible. Most of the conversions were of petrol-engined buses and

Glasgow Corporation helps out in London. Glasgow 43(YS2103), a 1936 Albion Venturer with Cowieson body, in Trafalgar Square in December 1941.
[London Transport

among the most successful were the more generously powered models such as the AEC Regal or Leyland Tiger single-deckers of the early 'thirties. But even with these models, operators abandoned the use of gas as soon as conditions allowed.

To return to the 1941/1942 period, the need for new buses had become urgent, and the Government took a series of steps to ease the situation. There was a serious shortage of skilled bodybuilders who were by this time often working on aircraft. The Ministry of Supply produced a "utility" bus specification, with spartan standards of seating and eliminating all panels having a double curvature. Upholstered seats were only to be available in the first year or so's production of double-deckers, and aluminium panels were replaced by steel. No variations on each builder's interpretation of the specification were normally permitted.

Chassis makers were permitted to complete such chassis as they could from sets of parts in existence. These models, known as the "unfrozen" chassis, were largely fitted with bodies to the Ministry of Supply specification, although there were also some bodies of pre-war standard, most of which were diverted from their intended destinations. Some vehicles intended for export were also sent to operators in Britain and among these were the first 8-foot wide buses and trolleybuses to go into service in this country—special permission was given for this use, the general width limit then being 7 ft. 6 ins.

A total of about 530 vehicles was made available in this way, mainly in 1942, the main types being roundly 200 Leyland Titan TD7, 92 AEC Regent and 85 Bristol K5G diesel double-deckers, about 80 assorted diesel single-deckers (mainly Dennis Lancet, Leyland Tiger TS11 and Bristol L5G) and 68 trolley-buses of Sunbeam, Leyland and AEC make that had been intended for overseas operators. These were allocated to operators by the Ministry of War Transport by no means always in accord with operators' wishes.

The next stage was a programme for bus production. The first types to materialise were Guy Arab double-deckers and Bedford OWB single-deckers. The choice of Guy was something of a surprise at the time, for Guy Motors Ltd. had not competed seriously in the bus market since the middle

Air-raid damage at Balham: a London Transport LT bites the dust. [*London Transport*

'thirties. The wartime Arab was largely similar to the 1933/1934 design in essentials, although of new appearance.

A Gardner LW-series engine was again used, but most of the wartime buses had the five-cylinder 7-litre 5LW engine although Guy would have preferred to use the six-cylinder 8.4 litre 6LW unit to compensate for the extra 15 cwt. or so of unladen weight compared to typical 1939 designs. This was again largely caused by the substitution of steel or cast-iron for light alloy in both chassis and body parts. Of the first 500 wartime Guys, only a few had had the forward-projecting radiator later to become a familiar Arab characteristic, and these did have 6LW engines. But when these, later known as Arab I models, were superseded yb the Arab II in 1943, the extended bonnet became standard although most of the buses had the 5LW engine.

All the wartime Arabs had a true crash gearbox, which sometimes caused a little difficulty in fleets by then used to easy-change transmissions of one kind or another. But the model was well received, partly because of the urgent need for buses, but partly because it was robust and notably light on fuel despite its weight. By the end of the war about 2,750 Arabs had been built, and the model outnumbered any other wartime bus. Practically all of these had 56-seat normal-height or 55-seat low-height bodywork of the MoS pattern.

The nearest approach to the Guy in numbers was made by the Bedford OWB single-decker. This was a wartime version of the OB model introduced in 1939, fitted with a bus body into which was squeezed wooden seats for 32 passengers. The nominal capacity was thus equivalent to that of many typical "full-sized" buses of the time, despite the smaller size and bonneted layout of the OWB.

But the Bedford was petrol-engined and this, together with its lightweight character, undoubtedly limited its appeal to the average large fleet operator. It seems that the authorities anticipated that the big companies and the municipalities would take large numbers, but in practice this was not so. The vast majority of the total of over 2,000 OWB models went to independent operators, although companies with fleets of pre-war Bedford coaches mostly took some numbers of the wartime version. A minority of municipal fleets took examples of this type. But by the end of the war,

The standard single-decker of the war years, the Bedford OWB with Duple 32-seat body.
[*Bedford*

OWB buses with their Duple-designed bodywork—some of which was built by other concerns—were a familiar sight, especially in country districts. They were often severely overloaded on normal bus services, but could be seen with loads of war workers, servicemen or even prisoners-of-war.

At the beginning of 1943, Daimler, whose factory had been severely damaged in the bombing of Coventry, returned to production with the CWG5 double-decker. This was basically Daimler's pre-war COG5 model with Gardner 5LW engine and pre-selective gearbox in wartime form. Exactly 100 were built before it was succeeded by the CWA6 with AEC 7.7 litre engine. About 1,300 wartime Daimler buses were built, including a small number of CWD6 models with Daimler engines, built from 1944.

Meanwhile trolleybus production had restarted with a "W" model substantially of Sunbeam design, but which was also sold under the Karrier name. This was a straightforward two-axle model designed to take double-deck bodywork equivalent to that on diesel models. Some 325 were built by the end of hostilities.

The final addition to the range of models available to British bus operators came in 1944 when Bristol restarted production with the K6A, a double-decker generally similar to the "unfrozen" K5G of 1942, but with AEC 7.7 litre engine. Some 250 of these were built in 1944/1945 before the appearance was changed by the introduction of the low-slung post-war radiator, although a further 52 chassis of the latter type had bodies largely of wartime pattern.

Wartime austerity ended gradually. The bodywork specification was relaxed to permit the use of double-curvature front and rear roof panels and upholstered seats at the end of 1944, when even the European war had some months to run. But it was not until some months after it ended that peacetime standards could be said to have returned, and some buses of virtually wartime pattern were still entering service a year or more later.

1946-1950: The Slow Recovery

J. M. Aldridge

The Prototype AEC Regal IV of 1949, AEC/Park Royal demonstrator UMP227. It was photographed here leaving St Andrew Square, Edinburgh, on hire to Scottish Omnibuses. [*Scottish Omnibuses*

In September 1948, I went to the first Commercial Vehicle Show since the war and looked at the latest type of London Transport RT on the Park Royal Stand. Afterwards, with a friend I went to Hounslow, the garage which was then receiving new RT's, but our ride on a 116 from Hounslow to Staines was on an ex-Tilling open-staircase ST.

This kind of contrast went unnoticed at the time and greater contrasts could be found elsewhere: the Omnibus Society had an outing on a 1928 Leyland PLSC Lion in 1949, for example, and Lions at that time were not uncommon. J. Fishwick & Sons, the Leyland independent, in 1946, had a representative collection of Leylands which comprised 14 PLSC Lions from 1927 on, 5 Tigers from 1929 on and 10 Titans from 1931 on.

Probably vehicle shortages generally were highest in 1947 or 1948; to help out London Transport and other operators hired 'coaches'—a remarkable collection of vehicles including Bedford OWB buses, a handful of old double-decks, and even ex Midland Red SOSs being seen in London. At the time I was at school in Hammersmith and very friendly with a driver of Smiths of Reading who, with an ex Scottish Bus Group full-fronted Leyland Cheetah, used to work on the 11 route. He and the vehicle went home at week-ends for coach jobs.

People tend to think of the war period as the time of shortages and utility buses, and of 1946 onwards being virtually back to normal. This was not so. Utility buses gradually became less utility in appearance and fittings improved. But there were relapses from time to time. For example, Cravens began bus body building with a rather austere double decker (Bolton Corporation had a big batch of them) and Scottish Motor Traction (as it then was) took some double-deckers with a surprisingly severe appearance.

The immediate post-war period was one of general shortages—of steel (which was on an allocation system), of linen for bus blinds, of glue to put the paper on the linen bus blinds and so on. If war-time traffic had been heavy and strained operators resources, post-war traffic was heavier.

Men had been demobilised from the forces and had their savings or gratuities to spend—and not much to spend them on. Cars were almost unobtainable, petrol was rationed—so was fuel for coaches, goods were scarce so that housewives did far more shopping (mobile shops were almost non-existent) and television was too expensive (and intermittent) to threaten evening bus traffic.

So traffic boomed, and there were no shadows on this horizon until the first fares increases about 1950.

During the war body maintenance had been probably more neglected than maintenance of mechanical parts, so it was not surprising that the post-war period saw wholesale rebodying schemes. There was a lot of difference between a 1928 and a 1935 bus, but after that design was relatively stable, so it made good sense to recondition chassis and rebody. Where vehicles were not rebodied, they were often rebuilt. Outside contractors were often used—Portsmouth Aviation, Mann Egerton and Marshalls are all firms who began in this way and later went on to full-scale bodybuilding.

Sometimes the decision to rebody brought later benefits—Ribble fitted oil engines and new Duple bodies to many coaches which came due for replacement most conveniently as the early underfloor-engined models came along. If they had bought new half-cab coaches after the war, they would have had to keep them rather longer.

One of the agonising decisions for operators was whether to order anything one could—even if it was not quite what was wanted—or whether to order a big batch of vehicles of a more specialised and desirable kind, and then sit back and wait for them to arrive. Many who were more particular bought a few standard jobs, just to tide them over. Big arrears in replacement programmes certainly gave opportunities for standardisation—Salford Corporation's fleet of double-deck Daimlers with straight staircases is an example that springs to mind: it took about four years between planning and receiving the first of them.

It is easy to sit back now and point out where operators went wrong. Perhaps it should have been obvious that the passenger boom could not last, but anyway most went ahead ordering, buying, reconditioning and rebodying. Some like Barrow Corporation ordered for years ahead to be sure of a place in the queue, only to discover later that they did not want all those vehicles. The post-war machine, apart from a few which had unseasoned or too-quickly kiln-dried timber frames, was quite reliable and long-lived.

On the administrative and operational sides the biggest cloud on the horizon to many was the British Transport Commission's area schemes, in which using

The AEC Regent III was a popular chassis in the late 1940s. This early 8-ft wide example, with handsome Duple 53-seat body, was delivered to SMT in 1949. [*Scottish Omnibuses*

Another Scottish Regent III, this time a Western SMT 1947 example, with Northern Counties 53-seat body. It was one of 58 similar vehicles delivered between 1947 and 1950. [*Travel Press* powers under the 1947 Transport Act, it proposed to take over all other operators in defined areas. By this time, of course, the BTC had already acquired the Tilling bus companies. It is often said that the unexpected opposition of the Socialist-controlled municipalities in the north-east helped kill the schemes. The first proposals certainly showed a lack of clear thought: United Auto would have been left with odd bits of territory outside the north-east scheme on the Carlisle side and at the southern end of their operating territory. All told there were to have been 12 area schemes covering the country, East Anglia being the second area proposed.

The BTC did continue with its buying policy and mopped up the SMT Group, the Red and White group, Enterprise and Silver Dawn and Hicks Bros. Also indirectly acquired were the bus operating subsidiaries of the Balfour Beatty group, following the nationalisation of electricity.

Certainly this period gave an impression of a virile industry—ever-rising traffic, more and more bodybuilders, queues, duplicate and triplicate buses and so on. The figures speak for themselves. Between 1945 and 1959 32,000 new buses and coaches were registered, and the 73,500 buses licensed in mid-1950 compared with just over 50,000 in 1938. Trolleybuses were 4,200 against 3,900, and trams 4,600 against 9,000.

Looking back at the engineering side one is struck by the enormous foresight of Midland Red, who launched into underfloor-engined single deckers years ahead of anyone else. Next came Sentinel, then the Leyland-MCW Olympic, then in 1950 Dennis, AEC and Leyland. Sometimes far-sightedness is rewarded, as with Midland Red. Sometimes it is not, as with the rear-engined Foden chassis announced in 1950. Another chassis ahead of its time, perhaps, but still successful was the Commer Avenger. The future double-decker was indicated by the prototype Bristol Lodekka which appeared before the ill-fated Foden. Even the popular AEC Regent with 9.6 litre engine and preselector gearbox was disliked by some as too thirsty and extravagant. Of course design must be looked at in conjunction with legislation, which planted difficulties in the way of the 8ft. wide bus, without actually banning it—it took SMT six months to negotiate for 8ft. coaches on its Edinburgh-London service—and did not permit 30ft. single-deckers or 27-foot double-deckers until 1950. Permitting 30ft. single-deckers rather killed the interlaced half-decker design that had achieved limited success.

There is a tendency to think of the British bus industry's faults and achievements in isolation, which is wrong. If we were running old buses after the war, so were others. It was not until 1947 that New York's Fifth Avenue open-toppers ceased running, for example. And in the immediate post-war period in Britain there were plenty of problems—like finding vehicles and crews to reintroduce express services. Southdown did this in style with a massed departure on different services from Victoria on March 22, 1946.

Two of the relatively rare Leyland/MCW HR40 Olympic buses, Red & White U850/950. They are seen at Abergavenny bus station. [*John H. Napier*

Oxford Street, London, in October 1949. Plenty of passengers, and a fascinating selection of buses to carry them. [*London Transport*

1951-1960: Prosperity and Problems

K. W. Swallow

One thinks perhaps of the decade of the New Elizabethans as bringing a return to some degree of prosperity after years of austerity, but it was the one in which the bus industry began to slim. This is no paradox. For prosperity brought a rapid increase in private motoring, in the use of mopeds and scooters, and in the numbers owning a television set. In 1950 there were $2\frac{1}{4}$m. cars in the country, in 1960 $5\frac{1}{2}$m. New car registrations totalled 132,000 in 1950, 805,000 in 1960. In the London area alone, television sets went up in numbers from a third of a million in 1950 to over two million in 1960. These were powerful social forces.

During the war costs of bus operation had been rising, but conditions then were abnormal. Services were curtailed and there was virtually no private motoring. Load factors were high. By 1950, services were back to pre-war frequencies. Revenue per mile was down, but fuel tax and wages, and other costs, were still going up. The trend was inflationary. For the first time for a long time, sometimes for the first time ever, fares went up, and soon increases became an almost annual event. Revenue

One of the coaching developments of the 1950s, the introduction of the Ribble Group 'Gay Hostess' double-deck coaches on Motorway services. A Scout and a Standerwick 'Gay Hostess' speed down the M6. The vehicles are 60-seat Leyland Atlanteans with MCW bodies. [*T. W. Moore*

went up 50 per cent but traffic fell nearly 20 per cent in the ten years under review. Passenger resistance added its effect to the revenue lost through motoring and television. By 1957 the industry accepted that it was slowly contracting. "Service revised" notices had become common, but invariably they meant "service reduced".

At the same time there was a staff shortage—it is still with us to-day, only worse. Full employment and the better conditions and more regular and shorter hours in factories meant that excessive overtime had to be worked by bus crews, increasing operating costs still further. Of course road passenger transport is labour intensive; wage costs make up 70 per cent of the total.

Vehicle maintenance costs were held in check, however. For one thing higher mileages were being achieved between major overhauls. The larger engines introduced after the war, such as the Leyland 0600 (9.8 litre) and the AEC A208 (9.6 litre), permitted departure from the traditional preventive maintenance and replacement by a leave-well-alone policy, where an engine was withdrawn for overhaul only after its oil consumption and general performance had shown this to be necessary. On the other hand there also began a trend towards lighter buses, sometimes—particularly in the case of single-deckers—with smaller engines, in the realisation that they were getting heavier and in a natural preoccupation with the aim of keeping down fuel consumption (fuel tax stood at 2s. 6d. a gallon for most of the period). The Leyland Tiger Cub and the first AEC Reliance single-deck chassis were products of this, and so was, for example, the MCW Orion double-deck body.

An early 30-foot double-decker, supplied to Ribble in 1957. It is a Leyland Titan PD3/4 with Burlingham 72-seat body. [*Burlingham*

The traffic fall-off started a general worsening in the quantity and quality of rural bus services. And for the same social reasons as affected the buses many branch railway lines and stations were closed. Under the aegis of the Transport Users' Consultative Committees set up by the 1947 Transport Act, alterations to existing bus routes were made and new ones introduced to cover rail withdrawals. It was said that about four-fifths of all the rural bus services in Britain were in any case then the direct responsibility of the British Transport Commission, which since 1948 had of course also controlled the railways. Often, however, British Railways introduced new diesel multiple units, but although bringing about an increase in revenue, sometimes dramatic and sometimes taking revenue from bus services, they usually failed to cover total branch passenger costs.

Politically the period gave some stability to the bus industry. The Tilling group had sold its bus interests to the British Transport Commission, and so had the smaller Red & White group. The railways were already nationalised. Though the area passenger schemes of the first post-war Labour administration, which the British Transport Commission had been enjoined by the 1947 Act to prepare, were still being canvassed as late as 1951, they never came to anything. Throughout the 'fifties the basic structure of the industry remained the same. Indeed, only now in 1968 is further disturbance starting to take place. The Conservatives, under the 1953 Transport Act, empowered their Minister of Transport, with Treasury consent, to direct the British Transport Commission to dispose of its controlling interest in road passenger transport undertakings, but the provision was permissive and the powers were not used. In two-thirds of the country the Commission controlled not only the railways but the large bulk of the bus services, and also had an equal or near equal shareholding in many British Electric Traction companies, until recently the other large sector of the company side of the industry.

From June 1950 the maximum permissible width of public service vehicles was increased from 7 ft. 6 in. to 8 ft. The maximum length of double-deckers became 27 ft. and of single-deckers 30 ft. Almost at once the industry began to press for double-deckers also to be built to a length of 30 ft., but it was not until July 1956 that the Minister granted this. The country's largest operator, London Transport, strangely conservative in this regard, was to keep to 27 ft. double-deckers for many more years, and at the end of 1956 ordered 850 AEC-Park Royal Routemasters to this length for trolleybus replacement. It was not until the end of 1960 that the Minister announced his intention to apply the maximum length of 36 ft. and width of 8 ft $2\frac{1}{2}$ in. to public service vehicles.

Development of double-deck and single-deck bus design had been closely related up to the end of the 'forties. The 1950 Earls Court Show pointed the way ahead for single-deckers—a horizontal amidships engine position with an entrance ahead of the front axle, giving a greater seating capacity and making one-man operation more practicable. While for single-deckers the underfloor-engined layout became generally standard, the basic double-deck concept remained the same. The low-height Bristol Lodekka, available only to British Transport Commission undertakings, appeared in prototype form in 1949 and in production version in 1953, its basic quality being normal two-a-side upper saloon seating within the 13 ft. 5 in. overall height of the lowbridge double-decker, which since the old Leyland TD1 Titan had had a sunken offside gangway on the upper deck. However, when in 1956 the Lodekka was coming up to the 1000 mark, Leyland's prototype front-entrance rear-engined double-decker Atlantean appeared at Earls Court. Between then and the next show in 1958 it was evaluated in service and on test, and it went into production in 78-seat highbridge and 73-seat lowbridge versions, the forerunner of the standard double-decker of the late 'sixties. Daimler studied the market, considered the success of the Atlantean and showed their concept of a front-entrance rear-engined double-decker, the Fleetline, at Earls Court in 1960.

Meanwhile, Dennis were producing the Bristol Lodekka under licence as their Loline, and AEC brought out an open-market version of the integral London Routemaster and called it the Bridgemaster. Guy staked their all on the advanced front-entrance front-engined Wulfrunian, but their development costs were not to be recouped, the company's overdraft increased and they were later taken over by Jaguar. Leyland, AEC, Daimler and Guy all continued to offer their "conventional" double-deck chassis as well.

The chief single-deckers of the period were the Royal Tiger and its lightweight counterpart, the Tiger Cub, from Leyland, and the Regal IV and its Tiger Cub equivalent, the Reliance, from AEC—and of course the Bristols produced for the British Transport Commission companies. All used the underfloor-engined layout. Bedford still monopolised the light duty and coach market, its petrol normal-control OB being replaced by the larger forward-control SB range, still with forward engine but gradually becoming increasingly common in its diesel versions.

The prototype Leyland Atlantean, 281ATC, on hire to Ribble in Liverpool in October 1956, a few weeks after it was the star of the 1956 Commercial Show. [K. W. Swallow

Integral construction never really caught hold of the British market—it still has not—and those examples, such as the AEC-Park Royal Monocoach, the Leyland-MCW Olympic and Olympian, the Beadle-Commer, the Harrington Contender and the Bristol-ECW, that were produced in the 'fifties did not have long production runs, though the Leyland-MCW vehicles in particular sold well overseas. Midland Red remained faithful to their own integrally constructed single-deckers and double-deckers and pioneered many improvements in design, and London's Routemaster, with its front and rear sub-frames, has been an outstanding integral double-decker.

By the mid-fifties there was no tramcar-operating town or city without an abandonment policy. Even parts of the Blackpool system were under sentence. From September 1950 to September 1960 trams went down in number from 4,610 to 677. By October 1960 when the Sheffield system was abandoned, only Blackpool and Glasgow were left. The once large systems at London, Birmingham, Liverpool, Leeds, Newcastle, Edinburgh and Belfast all finished in the 'fifties. Abandonment of the first passenger-carrying railway in the world, the Swansea & Mumbles, operated in later years by 106-seat tramcars, took place at the beginning of 1960.

Trolleybuses, too, were generally on the decline. They were "materially less efficient" said a Manchester report in 1953 (though retained there for many years afterwards), and it was no surprise the following year when London Transport announced its intention of replacing the largest trolleybus fleet in the world, a conversion programme that began in March 1959. In most trolleybus undertakings, peripheral housing development, traffic

management schemes and the high cost of electric traction were hastening their replacement by motor-buses.

In the field of express services the picture was much more one of expansion and development. Associated Motorways came of age. Created in 1934 to pool express services run by Black & White, Red & White, Bristol, Royal Blue, Midland Red and United Counties, it carried 700,000 passengers in its first twelve months; in 1955 it carried two million and is ever widening its network.

The first 73-mile section of the M1 motorway opened in November 1959 and immediately Midland Red began its Birmingham-London motorway service, using special CM5T coaches capable of over 80 m.p.h., equipped with toilets and offering end to end journey times of 1 hr. 55 min. at an ordinary return fare of 21s. 3d., compared with the railway's second class ordinary return of 2 gns. Between November 1958 and November 1959, influenced as well by the coincidental cut in rail facilities on the Birmingham-Coventry-Rugby-London line in readiness for electrification work, Midland Red's through Birmingham-London traffic went up 900 per cent. In 1960 Ribble and its Standerwick subsidiary introduced double-deck "Gay Hostess" Atlantean coaches with toilets, serveries and stewardesses on some express services, including a considerable amount of route mileage on motorways.

Earlier in the 'fifties, too, there had been an interesting, but this time short-lived excursion into the "prestige" luxury express field, when Northern Roadways of Glasgow ran overnight coach services from London to Glasgow and Edinburgh, offering light meals served on the coach and toilet facilities. The fare in this case was about 25 per cent above parallel services.

A more localised development took place when Northern General put on a group of limited-stop interurban services in 1959, some in direct competition with good rail services.

Extended tours by coach, now including a good deal of "fantail" operation centred on one or two resorts as well as the progressive type of tour, grew in popularity. The first coach-air tours in any quantity operated in 1954, crossing the channel by air instead of by water. Leave coaches for service personnel were a common week-end sight, gradually decreasing in number as military establishments were run down or closed. The introduction of coach rallies, now annual events at Brighton and Blackpool, belongs to the 'fifties.

The 'fifties were, however, the years when the industry first found its prime concern to be its continued viability, in a situation of staff shortages, wage awards, private motoring and television. But it certainly increased its efficiency—it had to.

FACING PAGE: Part of the large fleet of AEC Regal IV/Alexander 30-seaters supplied to Scottish Omnibuses in 1951 pose for the cameraman on the northward journey from London to Edinburgh. THIS PAGE: Two AEC/Park Royals of the 1950s. The AEC/Park Royal intergral Monocoach (top) belongs to Scottish Omnibuses, while the AEC Regent V/Park Royal (above) is owned by Newcastle Corporation.
[Scottish Omnibuses; Gavin Booth

The 1960s: Changes all Round

Gavin Booth

Changes all round—the theme of the 1960s. Changes in the structure of the industry. Changes in vehicle layout. Changes in passenger movements. And there are greater changes to come, as the Government's proposals under the Transport Bill have yet to come into effect, and will undoubtedly greatly alter the face of the bus industry.

The continuing decline in passengers, and the continuing lack of suitable bus crews forced the bus industry to take a cold look at itself, and where some operators had dismissed the whole thing as "inevitable", others set out to salvage the healthy part of their operations and took steps to stop the rot that was setting in to the rest. Many saw one-man operation as the answer, and set about converting existing vehicles for one-manning. Sometimes this was enough to give the kiss-of-life to ailing rural routes—but often it had been left too late. One-man operation has always been around, but many larger operators shied clear of it until it was almost too late. Large company concerns were the most suspicious, and it is remarkable to consider that the Scottish Bus Group, for instance, with a good proportion of low revenue routes in the Borders and in the north, only really investigated OMO during the 1960s. Some urban operators tried more ambitious schemes on a fairly large scale. Sunderland Corporation designed two-door rear-engined single-deckers to accept special prepurchased tokens, but the scheme was a

Daimler triumphed at the 1967 Blackpool and Brighton Coach Rallies. The Black and White Daimler Roadliner/Plaxton on the left won the Coach of the Year award at both Rallies, while the Roadliner/Plaxton of Evan Evans on the right was runner-up. [Daimler failure. London Transport, on the other hand, placed their faith in their "Red Arrows", again two-door rear-engined single-deckers, but operated on a 6d. flat-fare basis, with turnstiles inside the saloon released only by sixpences. The Red Arrows *have* been successful, and a similar system figures in the report *Reshaping London's Bus Services,* which is being implemented at the moment.

One-man *double*-deckers made their debut in 1966 when Great Yarmouth and Brighton Corporations placed PAYE Leylands in service. Many municipalities now look to the one-man double-decker to cut their losses, and, in anticipation, many two-door rear-engined double-deckers are currently on order or in service.

Even drastic surgery has failed to save many services, and time and time again operators have found it quite impossible to retain some services. Following the overtime ban in 1966 London Transport made many service revisions and cuts. In some cases independent operators have stepped in to keep the services going, but some have only confirmed London Transport's findings, and have fallen by the wayside.

The industry itself is presently undergoing great changes. The plans for Passenger Transport Authorities, first announced in 1966, suggest that urban services in each of four areas, Birmingham, Manchester, Merseyside and Tyneside, should come under a single authority. If these plans are carried through—and there is great opposition from all sides—there will be further PTAs in selected areas. Glasgow, one of the centres with a fairly complicated network of services, could be a PTA candidate, but a possible link between Glasgow Corporation and the Scottish Bus Group, first proposed in 1966, could achieve the same ends.

In the 1950s the organisation of the industry had remained fairly stable, but things started happening in the 1960s. In 1962 the British Transport Commission bus interests became the Transport Holding Company, controlling the Tilling and Scottish groups, along with the BTC road haulage, shipping, manufacturing and travel interests. The British Electric Traction Group, the other leading force in the company bus world, sold out to the THC in 1967 for £35m., and shortly afterwards details of the Government White Paper on Public Transport were first revealed. The proposals covering company buses included the formation of the National Bus Company, covering the English and Welsh company interests, while the Scottish Bus Group and MacBraynes would come under the Scottish Transport Group.

Many familiar names disappeared from the bus scene, selling out for various reasons to larger concerns. These were among the main acquisitions: Scout, Preston to Ribble, 1961; Baxter, Airdrie to Scottish Omnibuses, 1962; Moore, Kelvedon to Eastern National, 1963; Silver Star, Porton Down to Wilts and Dorset, 1963; Stark, Dunbar to Scottish Omnibuses, 1964; Carmichael, Glenboig to Alexander (Midland), 1966; Smith, Grantown-on-Spey to Highland Omnibuses, 1966; Burnett, Mintlaw and Simpson, Rosehearty to Alexander (Northern), 1966; Wilkinson, Sedgefield to United, 1967; Hall, South Shields to Barton Transport, 1967; Ledgard, Leeds to West Yorkshire, 1967; West Riding, Pontefract to THC, 1967. Most have disappeared into anonymity, but Scottish Omnibuses felt that public goodwill was important enough to retain the 'Baxters' and 'Starks' fleetnames and colours.

Elsewhere the ranks of trolleybuses and tramcars were being eaten into. Trolleybuses gave way to buses at Grimsby-Cleethorpes (1960), Bolton/Mexborough & Swinton (1961), London (1962), Doncaster/Ipswich/Portsmouth (1963), Hull/South Shields (1964), Rotherham (1965), Ashton / Manchester / Newcastle / Nottingham (1966), Derby / Glasgow / Maid-

Birmingham Corporation's standard design of the 1960s. A 1966 Daimler Fleetline with Park Royal body in Corporation Street. [*T. W. Moore*

stone / Wolverhampton (1967) and Belfast (1968). At Glasgow, the last British stronghold of street tramways, the tramcar disappeared in 1962. Now only Blackpool's seaside tramcars remain.

In 1960 AEC, Bristol, Daimler, Dennis, Guy and Leyland—all quite independent firms—led the field in building full-sized heavy passenger chassis. By 1968 most of them were linked under the British Leyland Motor Corporation. Jaguar Cars acquired Daimler in 1960, and Guy in 1961. Leyland acquired AEC in 1962, and an interest in Bristol in 1965. Jaguar merged with the BMC to form British Motor Holdings in 1966, and in 1968 Leyland and BMH merged to form BLMH. This left Dennis—now concentrating on goods vehicles. Bedford, long established leaders in the lightweight coach market, retained their lead, and their competitors of the 1950s, Commer, largely disappeared from the coach market and Thames took their place in the 1960s. So with the heavy market all-British, the lightweight market is divided between the two American giants, General Motors and Ford.

Vehicle types and sizes have changed drastically over the 1960s. The rear-engined layout has become widely accepted for both single and double-deck vehicles, and even Bedford and Ford are believed to be

developing rear-engined chassis. Daimler introduced their rear-engined Fleetline double-deck chassis at the 1960 Earls Court Show—a Show at which a London Transport Routemaster was the only rear-entrance double-decker—a remarkable fact when you consider that prototype Atlantean 281ATC was the only *non* rear-entrance vehicle at the Show four years earlier. Other new vehicle types to appear in 1960 were the first examples of Bristol's lightweight SU chassis, and Midland Red's 'home-made' D10 underfloor-engined double-decker, the first of two. After experience with the D10s, Midland Red fell in line with a good proportion of fellow BET companies and specified rear-engined double-deckers, 'outside-built' by Daimler. Midland Red still specify the underfloor layout for single-deck vehicles, interesting when you recall their pioneering work with rear-engined single-deckers in the mid-1930s.

In the 1960s the regulations covering vehicle dimensions were twice altered. In 1961 vehicles 36 ft. x 8 ft. $2\frac{1}{2}$ in. were approved, and AEC and Leyland were quick off the mark to produce long versions of their standard Reliance and Leopard chassis, which first went on public display at the 1961 Scottish Show. AEC showed a Reliance/Alexander for Scottish Omnibuses, and Leyland showed a three-door standee Leopard/Alexander for Edinburgh Corporation. At the same Show the Leyland Group introduced the Albion Lowlander, Leyland's first attempt at the low floor/low height double-deck market. Like the AEC Bridgemaster and Dennis Loline before it, the Lowlander never achieved the success of Bristol's Lodekka. AEC dropped their integral Bridgemaster in favour of the new Renown model, which first appeared in 1962. Guy introduced their first conventional low-height chassis the same year, the Arab V, which is still in production unlike the Lowlander and Renown, which were dropped following the Leyland-Bristol share deal in 1965.

The most significant new models of 1962 were single-deckers, like the Bristol RE, the first of the new breed of rear-engined single-deckers. Bedford got round the problems of a lightweight 36-foot chassis with their twin-steering six-wheel VAL. Dodge had a stab at the PSV market with the S306 bus, which never quite made it. Daimler exhibited a prototype rear-engined single-deck chassis at the 1962 Show, but this was to undergo changes before reappearing as the Roadliner in 1964. At the same Show Strachans marked their return to the PSV bodybuilding market, and Metropolitan-Cammell made an unsuccessful bid to compete in the light coach body market. Remember the Amethyst and Topaz?

1963 was a Scottish Show year, and consequently manufacturers avoided new model announcements. As a Scottish firm, Albion have tended to do the opposite, and introduced the Viking VK41L chassis with forward engine and set-back front axle, rather like the unfortunate Dodge. Thames also took the opportunity to introduce their 36-foot chassis, the Thames 36. Unlike their rivals, Bedford, they had found it possible to make the 36 a four-wheel chassis.

The manufacturers had good reason for biding their time, and the 1964 Show marked an important turning-point in single-deck chassis design. This was the Show when the rear-engined single-decker really came into its own, with the introduction of the AEC Swift, Daimler Roadliner and Leyland Panther and Panther Cub. Albion followed the rear-engine trend with a revised Viking, the VK43L, first shown at the 1965 Scottish Show. Bedford and Ford, on the other hand, stuck to forward-mounted engines with their VAM and R192 models, each featuring a set-back front axle.

Bristol made a welcome re-appearance at Earls Court in 1966 and stole the Show with their rear-engined VR double-deck chassis, but most other 'new' chassis were really developments of existing models, like

Longer double-deckers started to appear in the 1960s, like this 33-foot Daimler Fleetline with 83-seat Alexander body that was delivered to Western SMT in 1967. [*Daimler*

a 33-foot Daimler Fleetline for Leeds Corporation and a 33-foot Leyland Atlantean shown in chassis form. The first complete Atlantean 33-footer appeared at the 1967 Scottish Show. 12-metre (39 ft. 4 in.) PSVs had been legalised in 1967, but manufacturers were obviously waiting for the 1968 Earls Court Show to exhibit any.

Body design made great advances in the 1960s, with notable coach designs like the Harrington Cavalier (1960), the Alexander Y-type (1961), the Plaxton Panorama (1966), the Park Royal Royalist (1966) and the Duple Commander Mk III (1968). Notable single-deck buses include the BET bus style, introduced in 1963, and used as a base by many builders, and the ECW body which first appeared on the Bristol RE chassis in 1962, and was given revised front and rear ends in 1967. Bespoke double-deck designs for rear-engined chassis came to the fore in the 1960s, like those for Glasgow (built by Alexander), Liverpool (MCW), Bolton (East, Lancs), Oldham (Roe), Sheffield (Park Royal), Coventry (Willowbrook), Nottingham (Northern Counties) and Manchester (Park Royal).

Some of the other notable events of the 1960s do not fall into specific categories. In March 1961 the small exhibits section of the Museum of British Transport at Clapham was opened, and two years later the main exhibits were first shown to the public. Now it is proposed that the collection should be broken up—an unfortunate decision. Luckily Glasgow Corporation's Museum of Transport, opened in 1964 at Copelawhill, seems assured of a healthier future. Also in Scotland, the vast Alexanders empire was split into three more manageable units in 1961, and the division was made more definite when, in 1962, the newly-formed Alexander (Fife) and Alexander (Northern) companies adopted new colours.

And the future? We do know that there will be major changes in the structure of the industry; we do know that the proposed incentives will mean more standardisation in bus design; we do know that one-man operation, particularly for double-deckers, will continue to spread. But it is difficult to prophesy much more. All we do know is that change is inevitable—and that there are exciting times ahead.

The Future: The Next Transport Age

George Perry

Britain is still travelling through the outer suburbs of the Industrial Revolution. Public transport is a 19th-century invention only partially adapted to meet the needs of the 20th. Our railway network grew haphazardly under Victorian *laissez-faire,* with individual company profits taking precedence over co-ordinated planning. Many buses in central London follow the same routes which the horse buses took in the 1890s. Until digging started for the Victoria Line, there had been no tube railway construction for over 50 years. The only new medium of transport of this century—the air—has hardly been exploited at all for urban traffic and certainly not in Britain.

Since the war public transport has declined in face of the overwhelming advance of the private car. This decline has in turn further stimulated car ownership. In America some cities in recent years virtually abandoned their public transport systems; many have been sacrificed to the motor car by the intrusion of giant freeways and vast parking lots. Downtown Los Angeles, for example, was strangled by cordons of multi-laned highways soaring over and under what were once the city's principal streets. Downtown department stores survived only if they had large suburban branches at out-of-town shopping plazas where there was room for cars to park by the thousand.

Some commentators have argued that cars must be eliminated from city centres either by outright prohibition or by road pricing—some system which exacts tolls to a steeply ascending tariff the nearer one gets to the urban heart. This, it is argued, can save public transport by making its use obligatory. Since the publication of the Buchanan Report in December 1963 a more conciliatory attitude has reached the planning offices. The car is becoming accepted as a social benefit—and the mistake has been the administration's failure to predict its dramatic multiplication. Konrad Smigielski, the imaginative planning officer of Leicester, says: "The car is a wonderful thing. There could be four times as many cars on the roads in 30 years. This is the motor revolution. It calls for revolutionary approach."

The Leicester Traffic Plan is the first to appear after a major computer-analysed traffic survey of the type advocated in the Buchanan Report. "It is a technique of survey invented by the Americans," said Mr. Smigielski. "They have not yet realised its importance. Here is planning on a quantitative scientific basis, everything justified and calculated."

Leicester, which could become the pilot city, a prototype for many other British towns, wants to spend £35 million preparing itself for the 21st century. "Leicester is the result of evolution," says Mr. Smigielski. "We want to preserve local character, local identity and add new buildings. An old town with new buildings is far more exciting, visually. The true city is a congested city—but not with cars. Pedestrians. We can't plan the city centre for the full penetration of the car. There can be unlimited use of the car except in the inner circle. I'm against negative means, such as police pressure. The public must have a choice. We must revive public transport in a new form. We shall have a monorail running across the city from a new suburb to the north. It could reach the centre in less than five minutes. It would not be wrong in the landscape. Emotional elements are important with the public. It would attract public imagination, put a case for public transport. It would be the Underground of the air."

A series of interchange car parks on the radial roads would siphon motorists off on to public transport. There would be three kinds of bus as well as the monorail—single-deck inter-urban express buses, double-deck district buses from suburb to inner circle and small single-deckers, perhaps for standing passengers only, within the city centre. Mini-buses have been operating with great success in downtown Washington. A new type of taxi would also work in the centre, a cheap, silent and easily manoeuvrable vehicle quite opposed in principle to the massive conventional cabs of today. In certain streets moving pavements either at ground or first-floor level would speed up pedestrian movement where congestion is likely to occur. Department stores would willingly support covered pedestrian conveyors between their buildings and monorail halts.

Meanwhile, London Transport Board, which administers the biggest city transport system in the world, has been showing signs of activity after a long period of moribund despair. Street congestion and lack of man-power have led to a serious decline in the standard of service. Bus passengers are fewer—the 1958 strike when the buses were off the streets for seven weeks did damage that has never been fully repaired. Until last year (*1964*) there was union opposition to most moves to introduce major service changes. But in the next few months the biggest experiment in London history will take place when 50 rear-engined front-entrance double-deckers of a type familiar in many provincial cities will be tried out in London against 50 extra-long standard Routemasters with rear open entrances. A. A. M. Durrant, the Board's Chief Mechanical Engineer for the road services, said: "We tried a front-entrance bus in 1934. The only big difference was that it didn't have a door. It wasn't liked either by drivers or by the public."

A view that may well become more familiar: looking towards the rear of one of London Transport's 1968 flat-fare single-deckers, showing one of the entrance gates with a coin-operated fare collection machine. [*London Transport*

"People want comfort, and we as competition to private cars surely can't lag behind the sort of standards they are getting in cars. I don't believe in cattle truck conditions. We are experimenting with standee buses for rush-hour travelling. It will be interesting to see public reaction. The bus of the future won't *look* all that different. It has to be a rectangular box containing x people in comfort. There might be mechanical changes—for instance when torque convertors achieve reasonable efficiency. In ten years the fuel cell may be refined to work buses. A bus will now last 20 years. We have gone in for standardisation and interchangeability on a large scale. At Aldenham a bus gets a full overhaul every four years. It might get a new body too, and be as good as new." The double-decker will stay in favour, he believes, because it is more economical in road space. Although the single-deck standee bus is common abroad, the double-decker is making a comeback. Berlin and Madrid never gave them up. Paris is now experimenting with one. They are on the streets of Turin, Lisbon and even Moscow.

Arthur Grainger, vice-chairman of London Transport, would like to see the bus treated as a privileged vehicle. Bus lanes, perhaps against the flow of one-way streets, exemption from right turn bans and the spread of peak-hour clearways to all the radial routes would help London Transport. Incredibly, it is not a specific offence to park at a bus stop and until all stops have road markings it cannot be made one.

(From *The Sunday Times Magazine*, January 24, 1965)

History Repeats Itself

W. Heath Robinson

'An unrecorded panic at Whipsnade owing to a spell of wet weather.'

Then there were nine

GAVIN BOOTH presents an Instant History of Britain's chassis builders

It is remarkable that in 1926, as Alan Townsin reminds us in his "Lost Causes" article, there were 29 chassis builders producing passenger vehicles for the British market. Now there are only 9 left, discounting the firms which now concentrate only on goods vehicles. Even this is not really a true figure, as 5 of them come under the vast umbrella of British Leyland Motor Holdings, formed in 1968 to unite the Leyland Motor Corporation and British Motor Holdings. British Leyland's plans to rationalise the bus side of the business, which takes in Leyland, Albion, AEC, Daimler and Guy, have not at present been finalised, but more obvious model duplication will probably be eliminated, and bus production may well be concentrated on a couple of names, say AEC and Daimler, allowing Albion, Guy and Leyland to concentrate on trucks. At the moment this is only conjecture, but future developments from BLMH will be watched closely.

Leyland's roots can be traced back to 1896 when the Lancashire Steam Motor Company was formed in the village of Leyland. At that time the company was producing steam lawnmowers, but soon steam waggons were being turned out, with great success. This success was short-lived, as the petrol engine was catching on at the turn of the century, and the company turned their attentions to building petrol-driven vehicles—but not before they had produced their first steam bus, delivered to the Dundee Motor Omnibus Company in 1900.

In 1907 a rival manufacturer of steam vehicles, Coulthards of Preston, was acquired—the first of many take-overs—and the Lancashire Steam Motor Company became Leyland Motors Ltd.

Between 1920-1928 Leyland first dabbled in the private car market with two opposites, the superb Parry Thomas Leyland Straight Eight and the remarkable Trojan ("It's weird—but it goes" said its designer).

Leyland's 'L' range, introduced in 1925, really established them as leading bus manufacturers, as this was their first range designed entirely for passenger bodies. Next came the first Tiger and Titan models in 1927, and until the outbreak of the second world war these were Leyland's main passenger models, originally with petrol engines, but from 1932/1933 with diesel engines as an option.

During the second world war Leyland were heavily committed to military production, and although passenger models were re-introduced in 1946, the first real post-war models did not appear until 1947-1949.

The old-established Scottish chassis builders Albion Motors came under Leyland control in 1951, and Scammell Lorries Ltd. were acquired in 1955, but it was not until the 1960s that Leyland's spectacular expansion got under way. In 1961 the acquisition of the ailing Standard-Triumph company was Leyland's first large-scale sally into the private car market. The following year Leyland engineered a merger with their main rivals in the heavy market, Associated Commercial Vehicles Ltd., controlling AEC, Maudslay, Thornycroft, Park Royal and Roe.

The Leyland Motor Corporation was formed in 1963, and the next addition to

A 1967 Lincoln Corporation Leyland Panther with Roe 49-seat body. [*Gavin Booth*

the growing list of members was the Rover company, the last of the big "independent" British car makers. As was Leyland's practice with such acquisitions, Rover were allowed to retain their identity and, to a certain degree, to pursue their existing model policy.

Leyland's crowning achievement was the long-rumoured merger with British Motor Holdings in 1968, to form British Leyland Motor Holdings. The Leyland contributions to the BLMH are all old-established firms.

An Albion Viking VK41L chassis on test in the Trossachs. [*Albion*

Albion is the longest-established, being originally formed in 1899. The first Albion vehicle was a small dog-cart, which appeared in 1900, and the first Albion commercial was a $\frac{1}{2}$-ton van built in 1902. Private and commercial chassis were produced until 1913, when the private car side was dropped entirely. The firm, which had previously been known as the Albion Motor Company, became Albion Motors Limited in 1931.

Albion bus and coach chassis sold in large numbers in the 1920s and 1930s, and many operators tended to favour Albion's traditional ruggedness, particularly in Scotland, where many large Albion fleets could be found. Albion PSVs continued to appear after the business was acquired by Leyland in 1951, but these have often incorporated Leyland units, and some have been developed for the needs of the Scottish Bus Group.

AEC Ltd. justifiably style themselves "Builders of London's Buses", for they had their origins in the London Motor Omnibus Company, who operated buses from 1905 using the fleetname "Vanguard". Soon they started building their own buses at Walthamstow, and when the London General Omnibus Company acquired Vanguard in 1908, the bus-building side went too. London General continued to build buses for their own and for outside use at Walthamstow until 1912, when objections from rival operators forced them to form the Associated Equipment Company. The LGOC continued to be the main customers for the new AEC company until the mid-twenties, as the majority of chassis were designed to London standards.

To increase manufacturing capacity, AEC decided to leave Walthamstow and build a new factory at Southall, and during the transition period, AEC joined forces with Daimler to form the Associated Daimler Company in 1926. ADC built a wide range of models between 1926 and 1928, when they once more went their separate ways. Some ADCs were wholly AEC, some were wholly Daimler, and others were available with either AEC or Daimler engines. After their re-separation AEC and Daimler continued for a while to build models similar to those built in ADC days, but in 1929 AEC introduced their most important passenger range. The main models were the single-deck Regal and double-deck Regent, names which still figure in the AEC range.

Pictured outside AECs Southall works, an AEC Swift/Willowbrook demonstrator, which was soon registered FGW498C. [*AEC*

AEC Ltd. was formed in 1933, and the company became fully independent of the newly-established London Transport.

In 1948 AEC acquired two well-known chassis builders, Crossley Motors Ltd. and the Maudslay Motor Company, each with a long and distinguished history in the commercial vehicle line. Associated Commercial Vehicles Ltd. was formed that same year as a holding company controlling AEC, Crossley and Maudslay. Crossley-designed chassis were built for a few years under ACV, and the Crossley and Maudslay names continued to appear on what were basically AEC chassis until the mid 1950s. Crossley played an important part in the development of the ACV Bridgemaster bus, but no "Crossleys" or "Maudslays" have been built for some time.

Two leading coachbuilding firms, Park Royal Vehicles Ltd. and its associate Charles H. Roe Ltd., became part of the ACV group in 1949.

Daimler and Guy, the two other bus-building firms under the control of BLMH, arrived there via Jaguar and BMH. **Daimler** dates back to 1893 when Daimler Motor Syndicate Ltd. was formed by Frederick Simms, who had acquired Gottlieb Daimler's engine patent rights for the United Kingdom. Three years later the Daimler Motor Company was formed in Coventry, and the first complete Daimler vehicles appeared in 1897. These included commercial and passenger vehicles from an early date, and Daimler buses continued to sell so well, particularly to municipal operators, that in 1936 a separate company, Transport Vehicles (Daimler) Ltd., was formed. During the second world war, Daimler suffered badly in the Coventry blitz, but production of military and passenger vehicles was somehow able to continue.

Jaguar Cars, also Coventry-based, required extra space for expansion in 1960, and bought Daimler from the BSA Group. Although Daimler private cars lost some of their identity under Jaguar, the long-wanted bus-building side was allowed to flourish, and Transport Vehicles (Daimler) became Daimler Transport Vehicles Ltd. in 1966. Later that same year Jaguar merged with the British Motor Corporation to form British Motor Holdings Ltd.

After the Daimler take-over Jaguar sought further outlets in the commercial vehicle industry. Guy Motors Ltd. was then in the hands of the receivers, and Jaguar stepped in and purchased the company.

Guy Motors Ltd. was established by Sidney Guy at Wolverhampton 1914, and built goods and passenger chassis. Like Leyland, Guy had an affair with the private car, and like Leyland the results were creditable—though short-lived. In the 1920s Guy introduced many advances in the bus field, like the first drop-frame bus chassis, in 1924, and the first six-wheel double-decker, in 1926. Guy were less active in the bus side in the 1930s, and it surprised many when they were chosen to produce utility double-deck bus chassis during the second world war. In 1947 the Sunbeam Trolleybus Company was acquired.

The firm, however, was not on a sound financial footing in the mid-1950s, and the costly development of the relatively unsuccessful Wulfrunian double-deck chassis only aggravated matters, which led to the appointment of a receiver in 1961.

One of the first 33-foot double-deckers, a Leeds Corporation Daimler Fleetline with Roe body. [*Daimler*

Guy Passenger vehicles are now mainly produced for export markets. This Guy Arab V was supplied to Hong Kong in 1966. [*Guy*

Bristol Commercial Vehicles Ltd. is really outwith the control of British Leyland, but Leyland did acquire a 25 per cent interest in this state-owned company in 1965, enabling Bristol chassis to reach a wider market. Although some bus chassis were built from around 1906 by the Bristol Tramways & Carriage Company, it was not until 1913 that regular production commenced. Initially Bristol built bus chassis for their own use, but soon other operators were buying Bristols. In 1931 Bristol became associated with the Tilling group, and supplied large numbers of chassis to Tilling companies until the war interrupted in 1941.

During the last years of the second world war Bristol resumed chassis production, with a wartime version of their pre-war K type chassis, and normal production restarted in 1946, supplying chassis to Tilling and non-Tilling fleets.

When the Tilling group voluntarily sold out to the British Transport Commission in 1948, the chassis-building side of Bristol passed into BTC hands. Sales of Bristol chassis were now restricted to BTC-owned fleets—the ex-Tilling companies, the Scottish Bus Group and, theoretically, London Transport—and Eastern Coachworks, which had, like Bristol, started as part of an operating company, built the bodies on the large majority of Bristols for seventeen years, until the Leyland-Bristol share exchange. The Tilling fleets were likewise restricted to the Bristol/ECW combination during this period, save for small numbers of lightweight coaches. The London and Scottish fleets were in a different position, being able to buy Bristol/ECW vehicles as well as any other make on the market. In practice, London Transport bought a number of ECW bodies for AEC Regal IV and Guy Vixen chassis; the Scottish Bus Group, on the other hand, has large numbers of standard Bristol/ECW vehicles, in addition to several Bristol single-deckers with Alexander bodies—the only non-ECW Bristol passenger chassis built during the restricted period. After 1965 Bristol chassis and ECW bodies—not necessarily together—have been snatched up by municipalities, BET firms and even independents. Some had been keen Bristol users in pre-BTC days, but some important orders have been won from operators with little or no previous Bristol experience. Observers who are concerned with British Leyland's virtual monopoly, are looking to Bristol to offer some keen competition, and to the two firms controlling the lightweight coach market, Bedford and Ford.

Eastern Scottish bought a fleet of Bristol RELH6Gs with Alexander bodies in 1966, for their various Edinburgh–London services. [Gavin Booth

Vauxhall Motors built their first car in 1903 and expanded rapidly to the mid-1920s when General Motors Corporation of America, seeking facilities in Britian, bought them over. Under General Motors control, Vauxhall first produced commercial vehicles in 1931, marketing them under the

A Bedford VAM70 with 45-seat Plaxton body competing in the 1968 Brighton Coach Rally. It is owned by Jack Wingrove of Hazlemere. [Vauxhall

name **Bedford.** Bus and truck chassis were built, and Bedford commercials enjoyed the same success as Vauxhall cars. From the start Bedford catered for, and soon cornered, the light coach market with their reliable normal-control chassis. The only single-deck passenger chassis produced for a good part of the second world war was the Bedford OWB, coupled with a Duple-designed utility body. In 1950 Bedford introduced their first forward-control passenger chassis, the SB, which became their standard coach model for the whole of the1950s, and in 1962 they broke new ground with the twin-steering six-wheel VAL 36-foot model.

The British **Ford** Motor Company is also an offshoot of an American empire, dating back to 1896 when Henry Ford built his Quadricycle in Michigan. The history of the passenger vehicle side of Ford of Britain really only dates to 1959, when the first 'legitimate' bus and coach chassis were introduced. Ford PSVs have appeared in small numbers over the years, from quaint Model T conversions in the 1920s to normal-control Thames truck conversions

A Ford R192 with Strachans body, owned by York Bros of Northampton. [*Ford*

in the 1950s. In 1959 a PSV version of the Thames Trader chassis was introduced, which was joined in 1963 by a 36-foot chassis, the Thames 36. The Trader became the Thames 30 at the same time. The "Thames" name was dropped in 1965, and the Thames 36 became the Ford R226, being joined that same year by a new model, the R192. Ford's only other PSV model is the Transit, which, like models marketed by BMC, Bedford, Commer and even Land Rover, is based on a small van chassis, and PSV conversions are carried out largely by a few specialised coachbuilders.

In postwar years firms which are still active, like Atkinson, Dennis, Dodge, Foden and Sentinel, have produced passenger chassis for the home market, but the only other British manufacturer currently producing bus and coach chassis is **Seddon.**

Foster and Seddon was formed in 1919, trading as haulage contractors and commercial vehicle distributors. In 1938 it was decided to commence production of a 6-ton diesel lorry, which remained in production until 1940. After the war the company became Seddon Motors Ltd., and they soon moved from older premises in Salford to their present Woodstock Factory in Oldham. The additional space allowed them to commence production of single-deck bus and coach chassis, and while many were exported, several entered service with British operators, including full-size underfloor-engined vehicles. By 1951 the firm had become Seddon Diesel Vehicles Ltd. Production of PSVs for the home market slackened off in the mid-1950s, but Seddon are making a determined attempt for a portion of the market with their Pennine IV chassis, which permits body lengths up to 36 feet. Seddon are also expected to introduce a rear-engined vehicle with body by their subsidiary company Pennine Coachcraft, and in view of the grasp BLMC have on the bus manufacturing industry, developments at Seddon will be closely watched.

An attractive Seddon Pennine with Pennine body, recently supplied to Jersey Motor Transport. [*Seddon*

Lost Causes of the Bus Industry

A. Alan Townsin, MI Mech E

In these days of standardisation and mergers, it seems almost incredible that over 55 makes of bus chassis were on the British market in 1926. A list published in *The Commercial Motor* of February 9th that year quoted 29 British makes (including four Scots), 12 from the United States, seven from France, two Italian, two Swiss, one Belgian and two whose origin I cannot identify. Some 62 public service vehicle bodybuilders were listed in the same issue, all with addresses in Britain.

Neither of these lists are complete. The chassis makes omitted SOS, the product of the Midland Red operating company, later to become known by the initials BMMO of the concern's full title, Birmingham and Midland Motor Omnibus Co. Ltd., for example. Admittedly, this make was sold only to associated companies, but as such it became familiar far outside the Midland Red area. The bodybuilder's list did not include chassis makers building their own bodywork, operators building solely for their own fleets or the dozens of small firms who obtained all their business locally.

ABOVE: The most lost of the Lost Causes was the Gilford company. Great Western Railway UL9486 was a 1929 Gilford 1660T with Wycombe body.
[Bus and Coach

Many more firms came and went over the years. In the early days, buses tended to be built on a one-off basis—in effect they were all experimental. Almost any engineering concern could have a go, and many of them did. Many firms never got beyond the stage of building a few vehicles, and their names received little publicity.

But it is probably true that the number of "lost causes" of one kind or another among bus and coach chassis makers alone is well over 100. It is clearly impossible to survey the activities of all, even if information were available, in the space available here. But the firms in question generally fall fairly precisely into specific groups and these groups tend to have a common pattern.

Perhaps it would be best to define what is meant by a "lost cause" in this context. The phrase was coined by Lord Montagu of Beaulieu for a book reviewing defunct makes of private car. So far as buses and coaches are concerned, it can be interpreted in varying ways. Perhaps the simplest would be to say makes of bus or coach no longer available. Should the words "in Britain" be added? Imported passenger chassis were popular in the 'twenties, especially with smaller operators, but a combination of economics and tighter regulations on the design of public service vehicles to be used in Britain cut off the flow fairly abruptly in the early 'thirties.

So makes like Chevolet, GMC and Lancia have been dead for 35 years or more so so far as sales of buses or coaches in Britain are concerned. Elsewhere in the world things are very different.

Then there are the concerns which once made bus or coach chassis but nowadays confine their production to other kinds of motor vehicle, generally goods-carrying.

Many household names belong to this category, including Dennis, Foden and, if we ignore vehicles in the minibus class, Commer and Morris-Commercial. Some, at least, of these may return to passenger vehicle production in the future. Even though this may apply to only one or two concerns it is perhaps premature to regard them as irrevocably "lost".

The hard core of lost causes thus boils down to the former bus or coach chassis-makers who no longer produce any kind of motor vehicle. Most of these have gone out of business entirely, but some survive as factories or even companies in the groups that took them over, making parts or units, some of which may still be used in buses or coaches.

This Thornycroft Daring was one of the large Thornycroft fleet operated by Perth Corporation. It was new in 1933 and had a Metropolitan-Cammell 48-seat body. It passed into the Alexander fleet in 1934 when the Perth municipal services were taken over.
[RL Grieves collection

Working on the basis of this last definition, the 1926 chassis makers included the following lost causes: Auto-Traction (Minerva), Baico, Bean, Berna, Brockway, Burford, Caledon, Clyde, Cottin et Desgouttes, Crossley, De Dion, Fageol, FWD, Martin, Maudslay, McCurd, Overland, Pierce Arrow, Republic, Sentinel, Star, Straker Squire, Tilling-Stevens, Unic, Vulcan, W and G, and Yellow Coach. The foregoing were motor bus makers (except the Sentinel steamer), and, in addition, the following built trolley buses: Garrett, Railless, Ransomes and Straker-Clough.

Of these, many were of no more than marginal importance, at any rate in this country. I doubt if any but Burford, Clyde, Crossley, Gilford, Halley, Maudslay, Star, Straker Squire, Tilling-Stevens, Unic, Vulcan and W and G sold more than a few dozen bus or coach chassis in Britain. Of these, Crossley, Gilford, Maudslay and Tilling-Stevens were much more important than any of the others.

Their histories contrasted with each other, and although no two firms' stories are identical, examination of these four conveys a good deal about the others.

Crossley Motors Ltd. began in 1910 as an offshoot of the Crossley gas engine business (cars having been made from 1906) and, until the second World War, occupied neighbouring premises at Gorton, on the east side of Manchester. At first it was concerned primarily with private cars, but Crossley first became a familiar name during the first World War as a manufacturer of staff cars and tenders for the armed forces, becoming particularly associated with the early days of the Royal Air Force. Although an orthodox four-cylinder design of the period, it earned a reputation for refinement and reliability.

Numbers of ex-military Crossleys, like many other makes of vehicle, were put on the market in 1919 and a number of them was used as small buses, seating about 14 passengers. They had the distinction of being among the very few buses to have wire wheels. New vehicles of similar design were offered in the 'twenties but Crossley remained primarily a car maker until 1928. Then a full-sized forward-control single-decker called the Eagle was introduced. It, again, was quite orthodox for the period and did not make much impression amid the intense competition of the time. It has a four-cylinder petrol engine and better results were obtained with a six-cylinder version which, in double-deck form, was called the Condor.

The Condor appeared on the scene just as Manchester Corporation began to expand its bus fleet in the early stages of tram replacement and a large proportion of Manchester's bus orders in the 1930-1950 period naturally enough went to the local maker.

Other municipal orders were obtained and by 1931 Crossley had become a well-known bus builder, incidentally also producing the bodies for many of its products. But another factor was to bring Crossley even greater success. The diesel engine had first successfully been applied to road

A Crossley Condor supplied in 1932 to Barrow Corporation. It had a Northern Counties 48-seat body. [*Crossley*

vehicles in Germany in the 'twenties. Interest in the idea grew in this country and experimental Crossleys with marine-type engines built by Gardner (another Manchester concern) and supplied to Leeds and Manchester in September 1930 were the first diesel double-deckers to enter public service in Britain.

But Crossley could draw on its own resources of diesel engine knowledge, and before the end of that year had a Crossley-engined diesel bus on the market. Crossley and AEC, who in those days were in no way connected, were running neck and neck in the race to exploit the diesel bus boom which both could foresee, evidently more clearly than other British makers. For the next two years or so, Crossley forged ahead, securing more diesel bus business than any other manufacturer and possibly as much as all the others put together. Almost all was for municipalities and for a time diesel Condors outnumbered any other type of British diesel bus. Like most pioneers the Crossley concern had its teething troubles with the new venture. In retrospect, the early Crossley direct-injection diesels—always referred to simply as oil engines in those days—appear to have been fundamentally sound if not entirely trouble-free in practice and the principle of generous swift volume (just over 9 litres in this case) was later adopted with enthusiasm by AEC and others.

But Crossley decided to abandon the direct-injection system and go over in 1934 to the Ricardo indirect injection arrangement then being used by AEC. This was possibly an easier proposition to develop at the time but was fundamentally less efficient. Gardner and Leyland had by this time shown that direct injection could be made to work reliably and economically, and when AEC began, without announcement to offer direct injection engines to selected customers in 1935, Crossley was left out on a limb. The aptly-named Mancunian double-decker of 1934-40 sold only in very small numbers outside Manchester.

During the War years Crossley reverted to the role of being a major supplier of vehicles to the RAF, but a prototype double-decker was produced.This went into production in 1946 alongside a large order for single-deckers for the Netherlands Railways.

Post-war Crossleys were designated DD42 and SD42, with suffix numbers to indicate design variations. All had a new 8.6 litre direct injection engine but this still did not quite match up to its competitors in efficiency or reliability, or indeed to the quality of the rest of the chassis. Demand for vehicles was brisk, however, and Crossley sold quite large numbers of these vehicles. Municipalities were again the main customers but a coach version found a new market among independents.

Experiments had been made with easy-change transmission systems in the 'thirties and a Brockhouse Torque conversion giving fully automatic control was offered in 1946-48 but did not catch on. Constant-mesh gear boxes were used on most models, but a synchromesh unit was developed, largely for Birmingham Corporation, and it is understood that heavy costs were incurred. These are sometimes said to have played their part in the decision to accept the take-over bid the AEC concern made in 1948. Production of "genuine" Crossleys continued for about two years, although Crossley bodywork was still being built up to the mid-fifties.

AEC kept the Crossley name alive for a time and at the 1952 and 1954 Commercial Motor Shows vehicles of AEC design with Crossley name badges were exhibited. But this policy ceased and the Errwood Park, Stockport works (to which the company had moved before post-war production had started) was sold.

The Gilford Motor Co. Ltd. was a quite different type of concern. In little more than a decade it had risen to become one of the most popular makes of coach chassis chosen by independent operators and fallen again until it vanished.

The firm had started, like many others, in the motor vehicle mania of the 'twenties which could be compared with the railway mania of 80 years previously. Few of the commercial vehicle businesses started after the 1914-18 war managed to do more than survive for a few years producing quite small numbers of vehicles. At first the Gilford concern showed little promise of being any different to the others.

It began in London under the name of E. B. Horne & Co. Ltd., the original activity being the reconditioning and sale of ex-military Garford and Fiat lorry chassis. Then, in 1925, it was decided to manufacture new chassis to the firm's own specification but using proprietary units using the make name Gilford. The proprietors tended to favour American material, having visited that country. At first the vehicles built were orthodox and not particularly exciting.

But the key to Gilford's success was the decision to market a comparatively light (but full-sized by the standards of that period) chassis with a lively six-cylinder engine of American origin. There is little doubt that the firm was astute in its choice of engines, for not all such units were reliable. The chassis construction was simple and inexpensive with no concession to appearance on parts normally unseen.

The Gilford soon got a reputation as a fast machine, ideally suited to the intense competition that existed among express service operators. The reputation was quite often exaggerated and many of the tales of fantastic speeds can be discounted. But it was probably this make more than any other that help to put express coach operation on the map in the late 'twenties and possibly to a lesser extent, even the early 'thirties. The Gilford was certainly not the only relatively powerful coach available, and some of its competitors may have been faster, but the reputation died hard. Expansion called for a bigger factory and new premises were opened at High Wycombe, Bucks, in 1927.

Two basic models made the company's reputation, both identified by figures denoting the wheelbase length in ft. and ins. and suffix letters for the driving position—OT for 'overtype' (forward control) and SD, meaning standard drive (normal control). From May 1928 to the end of 1929 the 166SD and 166OT were offered, and they were followed by the 168SD and the 168OT. All four models had engines of Lycoming design, the 168 models being readily identifiable by the Gruss "air springs" which formed an auxiliary suspension to the conventional leaf springs at the front. They were mounted one on each side of the radiator and were cylindrical in shape.

The 168 models were available until 1934 although few were built after 1932, by which period they had begun to look a little out-of-date. That could certainly not be said of the double-decker on the Gilford stand at the 1931 Commercial Motor Show. It was possibly the most ambitious design for a double-decker ever, and even now its features seem rather futuristic. Front-wheel drive, opposed-piston two-stroke diesel engine, integral construction, ultra-low floor and centre gangways on both decks, within an overall height of 12ft. 11in.

It would have been a complex and costly project for any commercial vehicle maker to cope with, and was probably quite beyond the resources of the Gilford Motor Co. Ltd. (this title had, incidentally, been adopted at the end of 1926). There might just have been a chance of success had the company's income from the sale of orthodox models been high.

But the 1930 Road Traffic Act with its implied encouragement of take-over and the formation of London Transport in 1933 caused many of the firm's most important customers to vanish. The Lycoming engine also ceased to be available, and the search for a replacement of equivalent value was none too successful.

The last Gilford model that had any measure of success was the Hera single-decker. Slightly longer than the 168OT and of up-to-date appearance, it had a Vulcan 7.4 litre six-cylinder petrol engine as standard, but the largest single order came from the SMT group of companies for 40 coaches which were fitted from new with Leyland six-cylinder petrol engines removed from vehicles that had just been converted to diesel. These vehicles, allocated to the Alexander and Western SMT fleets, had bodywork by what was in effect the Gilford bodybuilding department, Wycombe Motor Bodies Ltd., which was responsible for the bodywork on most Gilfords.

The end came in 1936, and the concern was officially declared bankrupt. Oddly enough, a "ghost" of the old firm lingered on for some time in the shape of Gilford (HSG) Ltd. This took over some Gilford material and staff but was a separate concern whose object was the development of producer-gas powered vehicles. It was later taken under the Sentinel wing hitherto associated with steam, and thus there is a tenuous link between Gilford and Sentinel (another "lost cause" so far as motor vehicles are concerned) who had a brief spell of success as makers of underfloor-engined diesel single-deckers around 1950.

The Maudslay Motor Co. Ltd. could undoubtedly trace its origins further back than any other motor vehicle maker, for Henry Maudslay could be said to be one of the founders of engineering as a result of his work at the end of the eighteenth century. The Maudslay concern turned its attention to marine steam engines and its London works engined a large proportion of British warships in mid-Victorian times.

The motor vehicle branch of the business was set up in Coventry in 1903. Buses were included among its early products, and what is now the Scottish Bus Group began its operations when the newly formed Scottish Motor Traction Co. Ltd. put a Maudslay double decker into service in Edinburgh in 1906.

The business expanded, albeit comparatively slowly, and probably reached the peak of its importance on the bus and coach side in the 'twenties. It had always struck an independent line on design and in its early days had adopted the overhead camshaft layout for its engines. A new range of models with designations ML2, ML3 and ML4 was introduced in 1924.

Among their main features were a new four-cylinder engine, still with overhead camshaft, and frame side-members made from I-section steel beams instead of the normal channel section pressed-steel components. The ML2 and ML4 were normal-control bonneted models and as such tended to go out of favour towards the end of the 'twenties. The forward-control ML3 remained unchanged in essentials (although

New in 1931 with Ealing Direct Coaches, this Gilford 1680T with Weymann body, GW 713, is now safely preserved in its former glory. [Prince Marshall

radiator design changed somewhat over the years) and continued in production until 1934, and was listed until 1936. It was among the most popular models ever built by Maudslay, large fleets being placed in service by SMT and the Great Western Railway.

In 1927, however, a new and quite different model was introduced. This was the ML6, a 7.4 litre six-cylinder chassis of heavier-duty type. With its advanced engine design—it had two camshafts and inclined overhead valves—it was directly comparable to the original Leyland Tiger TS1 introduced at the same time. It found some favour with the long distance operators, but neither the single-deck nor the later ML7 double-deck versions sold in anywhere near the quantities of the Leyland or AEC equivalents.

This was a time of intense competition, and Maudslay did not succeed in obtaining large orders from any big company, or municipal fleets, between 1933 and 1939. A steady, if limited, flow of orders came in from independent operators, however. Most of them called for a comparatively simple and economical model, and the six-cylinder models were dropped from 1933.

An attempt was made to succeed with a more advanced type of layout and the SF40, of layout similar to that nowadays familiar on Bedford and Ford coaches, appeared for 1935. Mechanically similar to the ML3, it had the front axle set back to allow the entrance to be alongside the engine. Some 40 seats could be accommodated, hence the model name—and the SF40 caused quite a stir for a time. The ML3 itself was modernised in appearance to form the ML5, introduced in 1936. But sales were limited, and only about one chassis a week was produced for bus or coach operators during most of the 'thirties.

A surprisingly modern-looking Maudslay SF40/Duple demonstrator of 1935. [*Duple*

All but a few vehicles with Gardner units were petrol-engined.

During the War, Maudslay civilian production was concentrated on goods vehicles, mostly with AEC engines. This was the result of Ministry of Supply policy which introduced the AEC 7.7 litre engine as an alternative to the Gardner 5LW. This move was ultimately to lead to the AEC take-over of Maudslay in 1948.

Meanwhile, however, in 1946 the first post-war model appeared. The name Marathon had been applied to some pre-war ML5 models and the newcomer was the Marathon Mark II, which revived the two-camshaft ML6 petrol engine in combination with a five-speed gear box. This refined vehicle was the last "heavy-duty" petrol coach chassis to be offered on the British market.

It sold better than any Maudslay passenger model since about 1930, but was overshadowed by the Marathon Mark III, of similar up-to-date appearance but with the AEC 7.7 litre diesel and AEC four-speed gear box. By 1950 over 600 of this straightforward model had been built, more than all Maudslay passenger models of the 'thirties put together.

The Maudslay works, which had been moved to Alcester after the war, continued to make Marathon III models for about three years after the AEC take-over As with Crossley, the name continued and one batch of nine double-deckers of AEC design but with Maudslay nameplates, for Coventry Corporation, was built at Alcester. But gradually the name was allowed to die out and the Alcester works is now primarily an axle factory for AEC.

Yet another quite different type of make was exemplified by Tilling-Stevens Ltd. This concern was started in 1910 as a source of supply of buses for the fleets operated in London and elsewhere by Thomas Tilling Ltd. in much the same way that AEC was originally the London General Omnibus Co. bus factory. The vehicle designs were derived from an earlier association between Hallford, a pioneer maker, and Stevens, the latter having developed an electric transmission system.

This was much the same in basic principle as is used on the diesel-electric locomotive. The engine, petrol-powered of course on a motor bus of that period, drove a dynamo which supplied current to a motor driving the rear wheels. The system eliminated

LEFT: Maidstone and District No 79 (KL9006) was a 1924 Tilling-Stevens TS5 petrol electric. It is seen here in Maidstone. CENTRE, LEFT: VD230 was a 1930 AJS with Stewart of Wishaw body supplied to Greenshields of Salsburgh. BOTTOM, LEFT: A more recent Tilling-Stevens was Holmes and Smith CNO30, a 1934 D60A7 model, with Duple body.
[Bus and Coach; RL Grieves collection; Duple

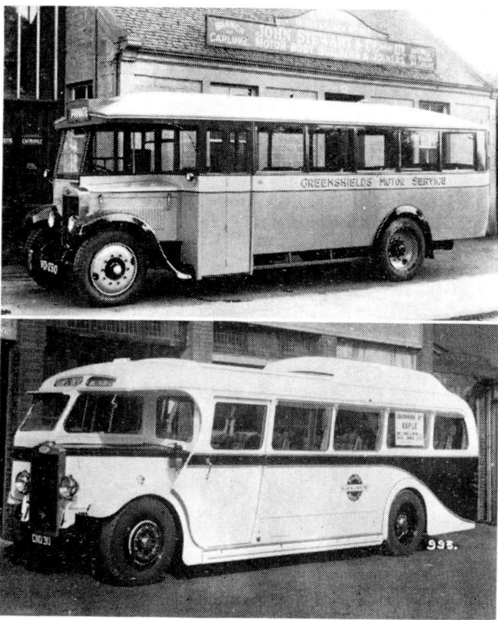

the conventional gear box and hence the need for skill in gear changing on the part of the driver. This was an important advantage before the 1914-18 war when experienced motor vehicle drivers were far from common. The Tilling-Stevens Petrol Electric bus had its full name emblazened on the radiator and was sold to quite a variety of undertakings outside the Tilling organisation. Space does not permit the inclusion of full details of the various petrol electric models with designations commencing TT or TS, but they included normal and forward-control single and double-deckers.

Production of petrol electric models continued until 1930 but tailed off noticeably after the mid-twenties. The electric transmission was heavier and more expensive than a conventional gear box. Performance was limited, although the smoothness probably exaggerated the impression of sluggishness in exactly the same way as with some later torque-converter systems. But more important was the greater availability of competent drivers. A demand began to grow for a simpler lighter type of vehicle, highlighted when Midland Red, then a large-scale Tilling-Stevens user, decided to build its own chassis with conventional gear boxes from 1923.

Tilling-Stevens responded to the demand by introducing models of their own with normal clutch-and-gear-box transmission in 1926. The first range, designated B9, looked high and rather ungainly like the petrol-electrics of the time. Demand for this model was fairly brisk, but the B10 series with lower frame and consequently more modern appearance, was probably the most popular group of chassis ever made by Tilling-Stevens.

With the formation of a joint Tilling and BET operating group, Tilling and British Automobile Traction in 1928, the prospects for Tilling-Stevens must have seemed bright. Many TBAT companies were users of Tilling-Stevens buses, and the B10 model with its 5-litre side-valve four-cylinder petrol engine was straightforward, simple, and by the standards of the time, efficient. The model name "Express" used for the B9, B10 and later derivations was perhaps a misnomer, for they were generally better suited to bus than express coach work (although the normal control models were favoured for coach duties by some prominent concerns, Southdown being an important example).

But in 1930, Tillings somewhat abruptly severed their connections with the company which then traded under the title TS Motors Ltd., the vehicles being known as TSM, until reverting to the old name in 1937. Tilling associated operating companies ceased to buy TS vehicles within a year or two.

Some attempt was made to obtain more municipal business, notably with a new six-cylinder double-decker, but met with no more than marginal and temporary success. So, from about 1933 Tilling-Stevens found itself in much the same position as Maudslay, and similarly found that its simple Express models were the most successful.

A few diesel examples, with Gardner engines, were sold. But in 1937 the company announced a venture which, for what had become a small company, was nearly as bold as the front-wheel-drive Gilford double-decker. This was the Successor, a six-wheel coach with amidships-mounted horizontally-opposed eight-cylinder diesel engine of Tilling-Stevens own design and manufacture. Not surprisingly, the flat eight proved to be beyond the resources of the company to develop, and the model, ahead of its time in many ways, never went into production.

A handful of orthodox Gardner-engined single-deckers intended for service in Hong Kong were diverted to the home market in 1942. After the war, Tilling-Stevens decided, perhaps belatedly, to fix its main faith on Gardner-engined models. Further examples were exported to Hong Kong and the home market six-cylinder K6LA7 coach did well in the late 'forties. Meadows engines were also offered and production continued unchanged for a time after the concern was taken over by the Rootes group in 1949. But business dwindled after 1950—Tilling-Stevens did not offer an underfloor-engined model during this period and the light four-cylinder Meadows-engined chassis which was the final development had little appeal against the competitive offerings from elsewhere.

Vehicle production ceased in 1955, although the three-cylinder two-stroke opposed-piston engine still offered in Commer goods models was designed and developed by the Tilling-Stevens works.

These four examples show how a combination of circumstances, over-ambition and/or timidity could eventually put once-thriving concerns out of business. It is easy to be wise after the event, but one wonders what might have happened if Crossley had stuck to its original direct-injection diesel engine and got the bugs out of it; if Gilford had resisted the temptation of trying to jump perhaps 40 years ahead of their time with the front-wheel-drive double-decker; if Maudslay had put adequate sales drive and development behind its 1927 six-cylinder model, and if Tilling-Stevens had retained its connection with the Tilling group (so that it would have been in the position occupied nowadays by Bristol Commercial Vehicles Ltd.). Food for thought indeed.

In Quotation Marks / 1

People have said some interesting things about buses. Here, and at other points in the book, we present some of the printable quotes, complete with suitable illustrations.

"They are ungainly, inelegant, monstrous masses of shivering tin. They are modern to the extent of being able to produce a perfect synchronisation of rock 'n roll."
[An Edinburgh Bailie airing his views on Edinburgh Corporation buses
The photo shows an Edinburgh Leyland Titan PD2/20 with MCW Orion bodywork, one of 300 ordered for tramcar replacement in 1954-1957. *[Leyland*

"This is the one British building to rival the great reinforced concrete roofs of Pier Luigi Nervi in Italy. The outside hints at the magnificence but does not reveal it . . . Probably the noblest modern building in London."
Ian Nairn on Stockwell Bus Garage in 'Modern Buildings in London'.
[London Transport

A Costly Failure

The costly development of the revolutionary Guy Wulfrunian chassis was undoubtedly one of the main factors that led to the firm's bankruptcy in 1960. The Wulfrunian was introduced in 1959, and featured an offset front-mounted engine, setback front axle, air suspension and disc brakes. This remarkable specification had been developed with the West Riding Automobile Company, who eventually owned 132 of the 137 Wulfrunians built. Two demonstrators toured the country, but most operators felt that the Wulfrunian was too much out of the ordinary to be a suitable proposition. The firms other than West Riding who did buy Wulfrunians either contrived to use them as little as possible—or sold them to West Riding; but now even West Riding are starting to withdraw their Wulfrunians, after a very short life-span.

TOP RIGHT: How it was done a Wulfrunian chassis showing the offset engine. CENTRE RIGHT: The first of the demonstration Wulfrunians, 7800DA with 78-seat Roe body, on loan to Glasgow Corporation. BELOW: An interesting line-up of Wulfrunians. They are (l-r) Lancashire United 58(802RTC) with Northern Counties body. Sold to West Riding and now withdrawn. Demonstrator 8072DA, sold to West Riding for spares. Bury Corporation 101(LEN101) with Roe body. Now sold. Demonstrator 7800DA, sold to West Riding for spares. West Riding 864(SHL864), with Roe body. [Guy

The Atlantean appears

At the 1956 Commercial Motor Show an MCW bodied Leyland Atlantean was shown to the public for the first time, and created a sensation. This is the story of the development of the Atlantean, a story which holds possibly more significance than any other for the post-war Leyland Group.

As far back as 1952, an experimental rear-engined double-decker was built for research purposes, the engine being placed across the rear of the frame and impinging to some extent on the rear platform. The small 0350 engine was used, and to increase the power and provide performance equal to that obtained from the larger 0600 unit, the 0350 engine was turbocharged. An automatic clutch and self-change gearbox was used, and the gearbox was driven through a more than right-angled transfer box and from thence by a short propellor shaft forward to the rear axle. A platform-type frame of steel and light alloy was used and this had deep sidemembers. Two of these experimental rear-engined double-deckers were built and were used by a number of operators for service tests.

In January 1953 a new development and research division was set up at Leyland under the leadership of Dr. Ing. A. Muller to design for long-term development. The general requirements for a new double-decker were laid down by the design committee and these called for a low-platform front entrance, so that the driver would have control of the platform and boarding and alighting passengers, leaving the conductor to concentrate on collecting fares from the larger number of passengers it was proposed to carry. The rear engine fitted in well with this scheme, but the need for highbridge and lowbridge types, the low platform height, and the desirability of keeping the gangway free of steps led to problems in frame design and suspension.

Designed as a complete unit by Leyland, the new double-decker had as its basis a fabricated frame with the body pillars permanently connected to the chassis outriggers. The chassis alone was strong enough to run under its own power, but the body was also an important part of the stressed structure and was built integrally with the underframe.

By 1956 the power unit was the larger 0600 diesel, placed at the extreme rear of the chassis across the frame. It was built as a unit with a centrifugal clutch or fluid flywheel, the Pneumo-Cyclic gearbox and angle drive. The radiator was separately mounted on the frame.

To ensure a low floor height, the drive was taken through the 72° angle drive with its spiral bevel gears to a double-reduction axle, the first stage being a spiral-bevel crown wheel and differential. Fully floating shafts then transmitted the drive through a low beam to twin helical gears which raised the drive to the centre line of the wheels.

At the front, the objective of a low platform was secured by the use of independent suspension of the front wheels with double wishbones and twin torsion bars.

The whole vehicle bristled with novelty. With an overall height of only 13ft. $2\frac{3}{4}$in., making it suitable for low-bridge operation, the vehicle with its 16ft. $2\frac{7}{8}$in. wheelbase had a smaller turning circle, despite an overall length of 29ft. 10in., than the smaller 27ft. long normal double-decker. Moreover, its seating capacity was increased to 78 without any loss of comfort.

Two of these prototype Atlanteans were produced, one being thoroughly tested by Leyland for some 200 miles a day of tough going over the Lancashire roads simulating service conditions, also at the MIRA proving-ground near Nuneaton. The second vehicle was put in the hands of a variety of municipal and company operators for varying periods for service trials and consumer research.

These service trials produced construction, noise and price criticisms which led to an intensive engineering investigation, initiated with the object of providing a framed chassis layout to make possible the fitment of alternative body designs with ready facility for maintenance and repair.

Leading the re-design team was Mr. John McHugh, Director of the Leyland Corporation Bus Division; and amongst the first decisions arising out of the design study was that, in the interests of simplifying production and thus reducing the selling price, the use of orthodox axle beam construction and semi-elliptic spring suspension was desirable. The abandonment of semi-unit construction and the use of a more orthodox chassis frame allowed a free choice of body layout, but the use of outrigger brackets from the frame to form direct supports to the floor contributed to the achievement of an overall bus height of only 13ft. 4in. unladen.

The noise problem was overcome by mounting the engine outside the body in a separate nacelle with a fibreglass cover; and the engine, gearbox and angle-drive unit was developed as a complete power pack mounted on a separate sub-frame. Completely self-contained with its radiator, it can, therefore, be run as a unit when removed from the chassis, by merely connecting up a fuel supply and exhaust pipe.

Another advantage for the fleet operator is that a spare power pack, pre-tested and fully adjusted, can be held in stock ready for installation. As was demonstrated, the complete power pack of the Atlantean can be removed in under ten minutes and replaced in little over fifteen minutes.

With the change to an orthodox rear axle, the opportunity was taken to re-design the angle-drive, which now consists of spiral-bevel gears from which the drive is taken through a pair of helical spur reduction gears which can be changed in size as required. With the standard rear axle ratio there is a choice of four overall transmission ratios.

Throughout the development of this project the Leyland engineers worked in close co-operation with the coachbuilders, Metropolitan - Cammell - Weymann, whose designers and engineers made an important contribution to the production of a vehicle in which the running units and the structure are entirely complementary.

In its new production form, the Atlantean was exhibited at the 1958 Commercial Motor Show. The result of more than four years' hard work and testing, the new model could be built with various bodies ranging in capacity from 73 seats in the low-height edition to 78 seats in the standard seating pattern. Adaptable to a variety of seating layouts, freedom was given to coachbuilders to meet operators' individual requirements; and, retaining all the mechanical advantages of the prototype plus a number of important improvements, the production Atlantean, at the right price, was an immediate success. Fully tried and tested in prototype form, the new edition was truly a product of engineering ingenuity stimulated by careful market research.

(From *Seventy Years of Progress*)

The final product: one of Leyland's own Atlanteans, Park Royal-bodied demonstrator KTD551C photographed in Glasgow on hire to Western SMT.
[Gavin Booth

Busman's Holiday

Tony Hogg

Daimler's demonstration Roadliner coach, CWK641C, impressed many of the trade papers when they road-tested it. Tony Hogg was also impressed when Car *magazine let him loose in it.*

They warned me that it wouldn't go like an E-type, but then an E-type doesn't seat 49 people not counting the driver. In fact what the fellows at Jaguar wanted to let me loose in was their new Daimler Roadliner bus. They said I could drive it all over the place, provided I didn't bend it and provided my licence had all the necessary clauses about operating vehicles not exceeding 19 tons driven by triple expansion, non-compensating steam engines with/without means for reversing.

The Daimler Roadliner incorporates a number of interesting and progressive features that are common practice in America and will probably be adopted universally in England before the turn of the century. The power unit is a compact American Cummins V6 diesel, which is built under licence in England and is mounted in the rear. The Cummins produces 200 bhp from its 9.63 litres at 2600 rpm, and 444 lb/ft of torque at 1600 rpm; 200 bhp is a very high output for this type of engine, and 2600 rpm is a very high speed. The equivalent English straight-six diesel gives about 125 bhp at 1800 rpm, and one of the reasons for the success of the Cummins is its oversquare bore/stroke ratio.

The engine drives through a fluid coupling to a semi-automatic four speed transmission, so that there you have two-pedal control even though the gears are selected manually by a small knob beside the steering column. This device looks exactly like the selector used for the old Cotal electric gearboxes found in Delahayes, and the action of the box itself is very similar. An additional feature is a two-speed rear axle so that eight ratios are available in all, but you are supposed to select the low range for ordinary driving and the high one for motorway work.

The test vehicle was fitted with a most elegant and comfortable Duple body designed for tour operators, and it featured air suspension although rubber springing is listed as an alternative. Buses are always custom built for a specific job, and Daimler is primarily interested in selling fleets for city work. Unfortunately in Britain these fleets are all bought by city corporations, which usually consist of a group of elderly amateurs, so that until you have tried to sell to the Liverham or Birmingpool corporation something that is a little new and a little bit progressive you have no idea what you are up against. In consequence some of the best fleet sales have been made in Canada where they evidently know a good bus when they see one.

Before venturing out in the Roadliner I referred to that factual but conservative journal, the *Commercial Motocar* just to see what the experts had to say. They described

The coach Tony Hogg tried, Daimler Roadliner demonstrator CWK641C with Duple Commander 49-seat coachwork. [*Daimler*

it in glowing terms as 'a wolf in sheep's clothing', 'the coach driver's dream vehicle', 'fast without being thirsty'—all this after having increased, for test purposes, the unladen weight of 9.5 tons to nearly 13 tons by placing 140 lb of sandbags under each seat. Thus loaded they got 0-60 mph through the gears in 64 sec. and 20-60 mph in top gear high range in 69.7 sec; the speeds in the gears worked out in high range at 17, 29, 46 and 72 mph, and in low range at 12, 22, 33, and 54 mph. which must mean something to somebody.

Leaving the factory we headed out for the M1 with a Daimler test driver at the wheel. We then cruised down the M1 at a steady indicated 70 mph (67 mph actual) despite gradients and a strong wind. The next step was for everyone to cross their fingers while I took over. Climbing into the driver's seat, I found the position very comfortable and the near-horizontal steering wheel of the correct proportions for the job (i.e. gigantic). The only instruments in the standard Roadliner are a speedometer and two air pressure gauges for the braking system, because it is apparently common practice with this type of vehicle to use audible warning devices for lack of oil pressure, etc., so that the driver's mind is not cluttered with facts until something actually happens. As far as vision is concerned, it is not so much vision as view—you can see for miles in all directions.

At idle the V6 engine has a characteristic beat; it tends to rock the bus slightly, although it smooths out immediately under load. Selecting first gear causes the transmission to drag so that the bus must be held on the footbrake or handbrake. First gear gets it rolling and upward changes can be made so that top is reached at about 30 mph. Changes both up and down must be made with an appreciable pause in neutral because a characteristic of the Cummins is that it takes a while to speed up or slow down due to some peculiarity of its fuel injection system.

With high gear engaged I soon found myself pounding down the M1 at 60-65 mph, and it is surprising how many cars you pass at that speed (you can hear the drivers complaining about the 70 mph limit as you go by). For motorway driving you have to plan any passing well ahead, and remember that when you give it full throttle the engine note merely hardens and the increase in speed is imperceptible unless you watch the speedometer. Another characteristic is that there is no engine braking on the overrun.

Driving on the motorway was a relatively simple matter, but the natural hazards of the highways and byways that pass for roads in England proved to be another matter—and a lot more fun. Surprisingly, car drivers, even Mini drivers, tend to give you right of way, although there are people who will baulk you going up a hill so that you have to lose speed, which must be infuriating to the professional bus or lorry driver when it happens for the 20th time on a wet Monday morning.

The brakes are surprisingly efficient, although they could be criticised for a lack of progressive pedal action and a slight tendency to pull. The action is extremely sensitive, and the merest touch at the pedal applies them accompanied by a loud hiss from the pressure system. However, the bus driver must use his brakes with discretion because if he applies them suddenly and severely he is likely to end up with 49 passengers wrapped round his neck.

The cornering power of the Roadliner is remarkably high, although I didn't push it to the limit. The steering is not power assisted, with the result that you cannot turn the wheel unless the bus is in motion. Power steering is offered as an option, but its main role is one of safety because it permits the driver to maintain control in the event of tyre failure at speed. The steering is positive with 5.3 turns lock to lock, and the only detectable fault seemed to be the normal one of beam front axles (the beam on the Roadliner looks like a structural member of the Forth Bridge); namely that undulations in the road cause wheel camber changes with a tendency towards shimmy and kickback at the wheel.

Summing up the Roadliner is difficult. One can say that there is a lot of it, which is obvious, but my main impression was that I hadn't had such a good time test driving a vehicle in years. Furthermore, after driving it back through Coventry and swinging it in through the factory gates under the discerning eye of Sir William Lyons I decided that if all else fails I could make a living driving a bus—and probably rather enjoy it.

(From *Car*, April 1968)

Background to the Bus Industry

R. L. Iles

Transport is a subject of considerable fascination: the proportion of the male population of Britain which has not been interested in some aspect of transport at some time must be very low indeed, and the rapidly increasing output of transport literature emphasises the fact that this interest is growing. This is understandable. Transport is one of the basic requisites of a highly industrialised economy, employing one tenth of the British working population to manufacture its vehicles and equipment and to operate its services; while over 20% of personal expenditure in this country is on transport and travel. Transport, moreover, is something tangible: the operation of a transport system can be observed by everybody, whereas of other equally important activities such as the production and distribution of power there is very little to be seen. Thus ships, aircraft, railways, cars, lorries, trams and buses all have their enthusiasts, some specialising in one or two forms, others taking a much broader interest in transport generally.

There is, however, a good deal of scope for specialisation among enthusiasts of a particular form of transport: some bus enthusiasts are exclusively interested in the vehicles themselves while others find a study of schedules and routes of greater interest; others concentrate on a particular aspect common to several forms, such as timetables or tickets. But wherever one's main interest in the bus industry may lie it is useful to have a basic knowledge of the nature of the industry and the conditions under which it operates. This article is intended to provide such a background.

The bus industry itself is a complex one: so complex, in fact, that the present Government feels obliged to tidy it up, under the apparent impression that such a state of affairs is indicative of inefficiency. Whether this is true or not, the fact remains that the intensive network of urban, interurban and rural services in Britain is, as shown by the most recent statistics available at the time of writing*, provided by 5,114 operators owning between them a total of 76,001 vehicles, in fleets ranging in size from 1 to 7,658 buses.

The present system of bus services developed largely during the second half of the last century and the first few decades of the present one: many of the urban transport systems began as tramway companies formed during the 1880s and 1890s and subsequently passing into municipal ownership; while rural services are largely descended from the general carriers who linked villages with the nearest railway stations and market towns, using horse-drawn vehicles more akin to wagons than buses to carry both passengers and goods. As the motor vehicle became more common, many of these vehicles were replaced by small buses (some carried bus and lorry bodies alternately to meet the requirements of passengers and freight separately), and this process was accelerated after the First World War when ex-Services vehicles came onto the market; during the following two decades most of the operators of these services were incorporated into comparatively few large undertakings so that by the early 1930s the structure of the bus industry was very much as it is today, with urban services provided principally by the municipal authorities (the tram was still an important feature of city transport although the motorbus and trolleybus were rapidly gaining popularity), interurban and rural services run by large companies, and a large number of routes in both urban and country areas provided by small independent concerns; the number of the latter has declined steadily since, though not nearly so rapidly as during the fifteen years or so following the Great War.

In addition to the municipal tramway operators there were a number of company-owned tramway systems: most of these were controlled by the British Electric Traction organisation, while the British Automobile Traction organisation, and later

*Annual Reports of the Traffic Commissioners, 1966-1967 (HMSO); the figures given above applied on March 31, 1967.

the Tilling Group, were its opposite numbers in the motorbus field. The BET, however, soon began to develop its motorbus interests and the BAT became the Tilling and British Automobile Traction in 1928, representing the joint interests of the two groups until 1942, when it was divided between them leaving, in addition to one or two smaller associations such as the Red and White Group, the main groups of operators which still serve England and Wales today. In Scotland all the principal non-municipal operators were associated with the Scottish Motor Traction Company, and this formed the basis of the present Scottish Bus Group, while in London most of the small concerns were absorbed by the London Passenger Transport Board after 1933.

The following table summarises the present nature of the bus industry in 1966; there have been some notable changes since then, which will be discussed later.
See Table 1.

Disregarding the jointly-owned companies, it will be seen that the existing operators may be classified under six headings: the London Transport Board is the largest operator of all and is not associated with any of the other groups; the Tilling and Scottish Groups, both nationalised (as is the LTB), and controlled by the Transport Holding Company; the BET Federation companies; the municipalities; and the independent operators.

1,803 of the operators owned only one vehicle each out of the total of 76,001 buses; in other words more than one-third of the operators operated less than one-fortieth of the buses between them. At the other end of the scale, however, the London Transport Board, with 7,658 vehicles, operated more than one-tenth of all the buses. A little over half the total is owned by operators with 200 buses or more, while nearly two-thirds are in fleets of over 100.

These figures show how the bus industry is dominated by the larger operators, which together provide the greater part of the system of services. Many of the smallest firms are purely coach operators concentrating on private hire, and, to a lesser extent, on excursions and tours: as will be shown later, private hire is a field in which it is relatively easy for anybody to set up a business since the only licences required are easily obtained.

We shall now examine the principal groups of operators as outlined in the table above in greater detail. The London Transport Board dominates the industry not only by its size, but also by its importance in the Greater London area: it has a virtual monopoly of all stage services within this area, although certain outlying routes have now been taken over by small independent firms who can operate such services at a lower coast than the LTB could; another reason for the Board's approval of such a change in policy was its own staff shortage

TABLE 1

Group	No. of operators	Remarks
London Transport Board	1	Also operates underground railway
Municipalities	97	Includes "Joint Omnibus Committees" (see text)
BET Federation	35	Includes subsidiary operators (see text)
Transport Holding Company:		
(a) Tilling Group	30	ditto
(b) Scottish Bus Group	7	
Jointly owned companies	4	Jointly owned by THC and BET
Independent operators	4940	
TOTAL	5114	

problem which was making it increasingly difficult for it to find crews for all its services—hence the pruning of parts of its system. London Transport itself is divided for administrative purposes into a number of sub-divisions. Administration of the Underground system is separate from that of the road services, which is organised as follows: the Central Area (running red buses) consists of four Divisions, each comprising two sections—one responsible for traffic operations and the other for running the garages and getting the vehicles onto the road: the Country Area (with green buses) consists of the northern and southern divisions, and is also responsible for the Green Line limited-stop services, most of which run from one part of the Country Area to another, crossing central London en route. The London Transport Board originated in 1933, when the London Passenger Transport Board was formed, under the London Passenger Transport Act, as a monopolistic undertaking to provide all road transport services in a special area, within which it had certain privileges and concessions regarding the licensing system. The large number of independent bus and municipal tramway operators which up to that time had provided services in this area were taken over compulsorily by the LPTB as part of the Government's policy, which was at that time to introduce much stricter controls over the operation of the road transport industry.

On nationalisation in 1947 the LPTB became part of the British Transport Commission under its new name of the London Transport Executive, which it retained until 1962 when it became the London Transport Board under a further reorganisation of the nationalised transport system, involving the dissolution of the BTC and the formation of two independent bus-operating bodies, namely the LTB and the THC. A more recent development has been to make the LTB responsible to the Greater London Council, resulting in a set-up similar to the proposed Passenger Transport Authorities, of which more will be said later.

Local services in other large cities and towns, and also in many of the smaller ones, are provided by 94 municipal bus-operating undertakings: the discrepancy between this figure and that quoted for March 1967 in table 1 is accounted for by two amalgamations in the North-East. In 1967 the two towns of Hartlepool and West Hartlepool combined to form a new Hartlepool, and the former Hartlepool Corporation bus fleet, comprising only four buses, became part of the much larger West Hartlepool fleet to make a total of about 70 vehicles; while in 1968 the new borough of Tees-side was formed, taking over the bus fleets of Stockton and Middlesbrough Corporations, with about 100 vehicles each, and the 40-odd bus and trolleybus fleet of the Tees-side Railless Traction Board. Other recent mergers have included Haslingden and Rawtenstall in Lancashire, to form the Rossendale Joint Transport Committee, on April 1, 1968; and West Bridgford U.D.C. and Nottingham Corporation on September 28, 1968. Municipal bus operators vary in size from 4 (at Colwyn Bay, where only a seasonal sea-front service is operated, using petrol-engined Bedfords) to nearly 1,700 (Birmingham Corporation), though the majority have fleets of between 30 and 250 vehicles: 67 municipalities fall into this category. Municipal operators in four conurbations (Birmingham, Manchester, Merseyside and Tyneside) are to be absorbed into Passenger Transport Authorities, which will be set up when the Transport Bill becomes law.

The scope of many municipal operators is restricted in that they are only authorised to run services within their own boundaries, though in some parts of the country, particularly in Lancashire, Yorkshire and the West Midlands, municipal vehicles may be found operating many miles from the boundaries of their own cities. These variations in municipal bus operating conditions are often attributable to differences in the parliamentary powers granted to the corporations concerned in the days when local authorities were either developing their own tramway systems or were acquiring systems from company undertakings which had been established in the towns for several years.

Also classified as municipal operators are four "Joint Omnibus Committees", all of which are in Yorkshire (at Sheffield, Huddersfield, Halifax and Todmorden) and, briefly, are jointly controlled by local and national authorities—the controlling interests of the latter were acquired when the railways were nationalised, the JOCs consisting of municipal and railway representatives; they are, however, complex organisations and merit far more detailed examination than is possible here. Certain other towns, as will be shown later, are served by operators working under agreements of a slightly different nature between the local authorities and a THC-controlled company.

The majority of the large company (i.e. non-municipal) operators were controlled until 1968 by one of the two holding companies, the BET and the nationalised THC. These companies owned all or a majority of the shares (and hence had control) of each company in which they had an interest; the BET, which is, of course, non-nationalised, also has wide interests in overseas bus companies, as well as in other commercial enterprises, quite separate from bus operation, in Britain; these are unaffected by the agreement mentioned below. The THC controlled, in addition to the bus companies, a number of other transport concerns such as British Road Services, the Thos. Cook group of companies, and the Atlantic Steam Navigation Co. Ltd.; it was, in fact, established under the 1962 Transport Act to own and manage all the transport investments of the former BTC except those transferred to the Railways, London Docks and British Waterways Boards. The THC also had since its formation considerable interests in most of the BET-controlled companies, since it acquired from the railways substantial shareholdings (though not controlling interests) in these operators. In 1968, however, the THC purchased for £35m the remaining shares in the BET-controlled companies as a preliminary step towards the formation of the Government's proposed National Bus Company, which is designed to control all nationalised bus companies in England and Wales.

The bus companies controlled by the THC can be divided into two groups, namely the Tilling and Scottish Bus Groups: the former comprised all the nationalised operators in England and Wales, while the latter controls those in Scotland. The Scottish Bus Group will not become part of the National Bus Company, but instead will form the basis of a new Scottish Transport Group which will also take over the road and sea services at present operated by MacBraynes, and most of the steamer services of the Caledonian Steam Packet Co., currently a subsidiary of the British Railways Board. In England and Wales, about half of the major operators are Tilling companies and the other half are BET-owned; even before nationalisation there was an "area agreement" whereby certain areas were allocated to Tilling Group companies and others to BET companies—involving some concerns initially in being transferred from one group to another in order to achieve a fair distribution of the market between the two: these companies are therefore often referred to collectively as the "area-agreement companies".

There are also a large number of relatively small companies which are in fact wholly-owned subsidiaries of larger concerns: these are often small firms which have been taken over by an area-agreement company, and which are treated to some extent as separate entities by the parent concern, often to preserve the goodwill which might be lost if the smaller company were to disappear completely. Familiar examples of subsidiary companies are Stratford Blue (of Midland Red), Scout and Standerwick (of Ribble), Altrincham Coachways and Melba Motors (of North Western), Sunderland District, Gateshead and District, Tynemouth and District, Tyneside Omnibus Co. and Wakefield's Motors (of Northern General), Durham District (United's subsidiary, which is now in the process of being "phased out" of existence), and Baxters (of Eastern Scottish).

A number of THC operators provide local services in some towns under an arrangement with the local authorities: in most cases the municipalities concerned operated their own services (usually with trams) at one time, and these were replaced by buses belonging to the company operator, but with the municipality retaining a measure of control by placing their representatives on the committees appointed to administer services within their area. Examples of this type of organisation are found in York and Keighley (West Yorkshire Road Car Co.), Bath, Bristol and Gloucester (Bristol Omnibus Co.). Other complicated organisations are companies owned and controlled jointly by the BET and THC: there are four of these, three being solely concerned with coach operation: Timpson's of London, Samuelson New Transport of London, and Black and White Motorways of Cheltenham; the fourth, County Motors of Lepton, near Huddersfield, was controlled until recently not only by the BET and THC, but also by an independent operator, the West Riding Automobile Co., recently acquired by the THC.

Independent operators are those which fall into none of the foregoing groups, and are usually private companies. Moreover, most of them are small concerns, owning only a handful of vehicles—as was shown earlier, out of the 4940 independents in 1967, 1,803 had only one vehicle each. The largest was West Riding with over 400 buses and coaches, but since its nationalisation Lancashire United Transport, with a fleet of over 400, has headed the list.

The bus industry as outlined above may, at first glance, appear to be a highly complex structure: but a closer examination will show that it constitutes a reasonably logical system. Broadly speaking, the pattern of bus operation comprises municipal operators serving the urban areas, companies providing interurban stage and express services and rural stage services, with a large number of independents to supplement them; many of the latter operators compete with the large companies in the coach field, particularly that of excursions and private hire. This is a stable pattern, and co-operation between companies is, in general, fairly close; competition between one stage or express service and another is practically non-existent, the real competition facing the bus industry coming from the private car and, to a lesser extent, from the railways.

It is evident from the foregoing that the bus industry is at present in a state of uncertainty: its problems are considerable and the Transport Bill is likely to bring about long-term changes in many of the features which have long been part of the British bus scene. But it will take a long time for the basic structure of the industry to change significantly—the Passenger Transport Authorities, National Bus Company and Scottish Transport Group will not immediately have a noticeable effect on the overall picture as presented in these pages, and many of the problems will remain to tax the patience of the bus operator. It has been said by some bus enthusiasts that the Transport Bill will take much of the fascination from the bus industry; but this seems to be a very unrealistic complaint. As the industry gradually changes—and some changes will undoubtedly be for the better—the intelligent student of the bus industry will have an unprecedented opportunity to watch and assess the effects of the first major policy change in British road transport since the passing of the 1930 Road Traffic Act.

In 1967 Hartlepool Corporation's four buses joined the fleet of West Hartlepool. A West Hartlepool Leyland Leopard with Strachans 45-seat bodywork is seen in 1966. [*R. L. Iles*

By any other name

J. E. Dunabin

The word "omnibus," meaning "for all," was apparently in common use in connection with the carriage of passengers by road before Mr. Shillibeer started running his vehicles on London streets. The need that was obviously felt for more precise identification soon led to the use of Mr. Shillibeer's own name instead by the public. It is said that this practice died when the same gentleman expanded into the undertaking trade. Since then, bus fleets and individual vehicles have been identified by the use of a bewildering variety of names, from almost every imaginable source, so that one finds diamonds, rubies, primroses, violets, crimson ramblers, and suchlike poetic fancies intermingled with names like "Barchester and District Motor Services," "J. Smith's Motors," and others equally prosaic. The name "West Coast Motor Service Company" does not seem one bit too grand or all embracing for an operator who runs for mile after mile down the west coast of Kintyre, within sight and sound of the great Atlantic breakers, but the journey can be made equally well in a bus labelled simply, "A. & P. McConnachie Ltd."

With such a profusion of counties, towns, villages, and even streets, flowers, birds, historical or mythological personages—and sometimes owners' wives—precious stones, rivers, and all the colours of the spectrum, it is difficult to know where to begin.

Where a business developed from the efforts of one man, or one man and close relations, then his name often survived. The best known busman's name of all is of course Thomas Tilling. When, however, a group of business men got together and decided to run motor-buses, they often followed the tramway pattern, choosing the name of the town on which operations were based to begin the title of their company. Barnsley and Bristol; Mansfield and Mitcheldean; many town names appeared in large letters on the sides of buses. Some disappeared as the companies expanded and altered their names to avoid misunderstandings, or as they were absorbed by others. It is, however, interesting to note that almost all the bigger operators use some form of geographical title, several, Birmingham & Midland, Maidstone & District and City of Oxford, retaining town names. What was the biggest fleet bearing a family name has now become three hybrids, with area names in parentheses, "Alexander (Fife)", etc.

Amongst the independents family names are naturally more prominent and town or area names are little used. At some point the distinction between fleet names and legal names should be drawn, but leaving that on one side, the reasons for the last mentioned fact may be pondered. Was it that choice of a geographical name went with too ambitious ideas of expansion, which rendered such companies vulnerable to competition? Was it possibly that these names, where they existed, indicated possession of a "territory", which made them attractive take-over propositions? Or was it that the take-over tycoons could only recognise who their competitors were, meriting absorption, if they had geographical names?

Within the geographical group, there are of course many variations. From towns some operators moved on to counties, one or possibly two (never three), while others preferred to use the names of rivers or river valleys to indicate the area they served. Points of the compass were studied, and much use was made of South, East, and West, with variations. Hills (Pennine, Quantock, Chiltern) have been pressed into service, too.

But what of the remaining words? "Omnibus Co. Ltd." is an obvious choice, but not as popular as might be expected. Traction was another favourite word, sometimes but not always ("Scottish Motor—," "Trent Motor—") indicating tramway ancestry. Transport was another. The use of the word "Tramways" died hard, but choice of either of these two words to succeed it would mean that castings etc. lettered "— — T" were not rendered obsolete. "PET," however, had to become "PMT".

Many companies used the unimaginative "— Motor Services" and a few favoured "Automobile," but the name "— Road Car Co." has fewer syllables and sounds much better. One assumes that this form of name, still preserved by several companies, came from the famous early London operator. Was there among the leading figures of the industry in its early days one who, whenever the subject of names cropped up, always voted for this?

Still on the subject of the latter halves of geographical names, there are the oddities, "Transport & Power," "Omnibus & Touring," "Omnibus & Transport," "Tramways & Carriage," "Motor & Cycle," and, a freak this, "Electricity Supply."

Then there are all those others, loosely described as "Independents." Here it is necessary to refer again to the fact, obvious but sometimes overlooked, that fleet names can be different from legal names, and can be treated differently. The latter generally remain for good reasons, but the former can be varied, added to, or even just lost, and can be shared by two or more operators. More important, they may readily be used as an outlet for the suppressed poetic or romantic fancy of many a rough, tough looking busman. How else can one account for the tulips, gardenias, and scarlet pimpernels, for Nell Gwynne, Robin Hood, Godiva, and other great names from the past?

One way of reducing such a bewildering array to something comprehensible is to look at different regions of the country. Rugged independence and individuality have not, it seems, prevented certain imitative trends from appearing. In Lancashire no common line is apparent, with Cadman, Corless, Dallas, Fishwick (all surnames), Grange, BBMS, Yarrow (three variants on the geographical theme), "Rocket," "Scout" and "Viking," these last three being of the fanciful variety. Other areas seem more promising. In Yorkshire, for instance, there were at one time, "B & B" buses, "B & E," "B & S," "EB," and so on. Initials serving as fleetnames were usually surnames, but not always. In the South Wales area, abbreviations used at various times have included AMS, EVS, RMS (two of these), CMS, SWT, and others. The letters "MS" stood for "Motor Services" of course. But in North Wales the theme was colour, with

TOP: One of the fanciful names—Scout. A 1939 Leyland Tiger TS8 with 28-seat Duple body. CENTRE: An Albion Viking VK43L belonging to Alexander (Fife) runs through the toll gate on to the Tay Road Bridge. The Fife company was formed in 1962 when the Alexander empire was split into three. ABOVE: Baxters of Airdrie is now owned by Scottish Omnibuses, but the fleet colours and fleet name are still retained as a goodwill gesture. This Baxters Leyland PD2/Massey is seen in Edinburgh bus station.

[Duple; Gavin Booth

"Bangor Blue," "Beddgelert Brown," "Mona Maroon," "North Wales Silver," "White Rose," and others. In Llandudno the charabanc operators also conformed to the pattern, with "Royal Red" and "Royal Purple," to contrast with the "Royal Blue" buses. Neither in North nor in South Wales does the native language appear to have been popular for fleet identification.

In the southern part of Essex, place names predominated. From memory, Rochford, Rayleigh, Thundersley, Hadleigh, Shoebury, Benfleet and Canvey were all used as well as Southend (Corporation) and Westcliff. Another local operator had to be content with the name "Borough."

But it is up in the north-east of England, in and around Bishop Auckland, that the fleet namer's art really flourished. What and where such a flowering sprang from it is not known, but here we have, or had, "Blue Belle," "Heather Belle," "Royal," "Imperial," "Elite," "Dauntless," "OK", and "The Eden," with the "Scarlet Band" not far away. Competition for names seems to have been keen; there was a "Favourite Direct," and a "Favourite No. 2"! It was in Co. Durham that the "Teesdale Queen" was born, and the "Gypsy Queen" too, yet the small independents who ran into Darlington, for instance, were not moved to flights of fancy in the way their counterparts were around "Bishop." But then, to hear a man in Spennymoor or Tudhoe talk about "The OK," giving to the definite article the pronunciation used elsewhere only when it precedes a consonant, was to realize that even a name like this could mean very much more than just two initials.

It is now nearly forty years since the heyday of the independent long-distance coach operators. Like swarms of bees they appeared, introducing a touch of something different into the business with their choice of identifying names. There were the "Albatross," the "Nite" service, "Eniway," "Autokoches," rather more conventional ones like "Morning Star," "Pride of the Road," "Majestic," "Golden West" and scores more. "Yelloway" is one of the few names remaining to remind us of those days.

Some operators' names—legal names too, not just those used for fleets—were precise, naming the terminal points. "Leeds Newcastle Omnibus Co." was one, and "Lochinver-Invershin" another. Some were or are vague and even misleading. An Englishman must not deny a Scotsman the right to have Midlands, in spite of the well-known occasion when two ladies, wishing to go to Birmingham, found themselves not in Crewe, but on an Airdrie-based bus. What, though, do the residents of Birmingham think of a "Midland General" bus company which comes no further south than Nottingham? Even bus enthusiasts for whom outer darkness begins just north of Watford must know the meaning of the word "Ebor." The company of this name ran in the Mansfield area of Nottinghamshire, and not into York. So far as the writer can ascertain, "Cambrian" coaches stayed out of Wales, and Ledbury Transport never entered Ledbury — where "Thackrays Way" ran—but then, Ledbury Tours Ltd., do not operate any tours. The recently departed "Highland" of Glenboig, whose operating area lay a few miles east of Glasgow, deserves a mention, too.

One could continue casting around, coming up occasionally with gems like "Enterprise & Silver Dawn," and "Sidmouth Motor Co. & Dagworthy," or speculating on a possible connection between "Auto-Pilots" and a name once seen, "Docks & Waterways Bus Co.," but a limit must be set. London, it will be noticed, with many unique and colourful fleetnames of the motor era and the one before, has hardly been touched on. The reason is simply that in the course of time—our London-born members having such prodigious memories (back to Shillibeer himself?)—every fleetname used there will be recalled in the columns of the "Omnibus Magazine". No provincial areas seem to have been so well observed. Let us not forget the "Comfy" of Ibstock, the "Cosy" bus a few miles further north, the "UNU" (U Need Us), nor, simplest of all, "Our Bus."

(From *The Omnibus Magazine,* January, 1967).

Sampling the Sea Breezes

The open-top bus is a familiar sight at resorts round the coast of Britain. On a good day it is a popular way to enjoy the sights. This is a pictorial selection of open-toppers, mostly from the seaside but with two 'intruders'.

ABOVE: A Hants & Dorset Bristol K5G unloads at the bus station in Bournemouth, after a trip from Sandbanks. RIGHT: Another Bournemouth open-topper, this time a more modern vehicle, a 1965 Daimler Fleetline with MCW body.
[Gavin Booth; Daimler

BELOW: One of the unique Southport Corporation Bedford QL buses with Rimmer, Harrison & Sutherland bodies. These have now been withdrawn.
[A Moyes

Retained by Scottish Omnibuses for Gala days, Processions, and cup-winning football teams, this 'unfrozen' all-Leyland TD5 is popularly known as "The White Lady". It is shown here bringing the triumphant Heart of Midlothian football team back to Edinburgh in 1959. [Scottish Omnibuses

A Southdown utility Guy Arab with Northern Counties 56-seat body, on Beachy Head. [RL Wilson

Liverpool Corporations AEC Regent tree-lopper LR1 (FKB337). [RL Wilson

ABOVE: In 1958 Maidstone and District placed three 1946 AEC Regal/Harrington open toppers in service at Hastings. RIGHT: One of the nine Devon General 'Sea Dogs' used in the Torquay area. They are Leyland Atlanteans with 75-seat MCW bodies, and "Sir Francis Drake" is seen at Babbacombe.
[RL Iles; Gavin Booth

LEFT: A Brighton, Hove & District Bristol Lodekka FS6G with ECW 60-seat body, seen at Brighton. *[RL Iles*

The Change

H. Webb

Pioneer busman Harry Webb was also an active bus enthusiast—even in his eighties. A few years ago he wrote a series of articles for "The Omnibus Magazine" recalling the early days of the bus industry, under the title "H. Webb Recollects". He died in 1967, aged 86.

The Tilling petrol electric TTA1—"one of those buses with a big nose". [London Transport

The Tilling organisation was among the first to utilise the motor for commercial goods transport. They built a small box-like structure on a landaulette chassis. It was hired by Peck, the potted meat firm near Old Kent Road. The coachbuilding department was moved to Salisbury Yard, Lewisham, but after a fairly short time a much larger works at Wren Road, Camberwell, was created and the Salisbury Yard premises became a motor-bus garage. At Wren Road bus bodies and various vans for commercial use were built. The company had been successful in securing several large contracts which enabled the works to be kept going at high pressure. Furthermore the later acquisition of various bus concerns all over the country meant that the volume of work could be kept up at a level ensuring that the full capacity of output was maintained.

Many business concerns hired their vans from Tillings. To mention only a few: W. H. Smith & Son, newsagents and booksellers; Cadburys, who one day called for and obtained 30 vehicles in addition to their already large contract fleet of delivery vans; MacFarlane Lang, noted for their biscuits; Vickers, in the newspaper world; Barclay Perkins, brewers, and many others. About this time Tillings owned several old vehicles which were hired by film companies and used in such productions as The Wandering Jew, Old Curiosity Shop, Nell Gwynn, John Peel, The Iron Duke, The Dictator, The Private Secretary and others. In the last named film a pack of hounds, huntsmen and whippers-in were supplied in addition to sundry vehicles.

Tillings built their own luxury coaches, including those carrying passengers to and from the airport at Croydon in the heyday of Imperial Airways. The absorption of the Daimler Hire Company by Tillings meant that over 400 private vehicles were available for hire. There is the story of a customer who hired a car from Daimler Hire but didn't like the chauffeur so she transferred her next order to Tillings only to find the car arrived with the same driver.

When we look at the London bus of today with the shelter afforded to the driver and the conductor, it is difficult to visualise that these men were exposed to the vagaries of the weather in the horse-bus era; indeed in the days of the knife-board bus the poor conductor occupied a precarious stand on a small platform at the back of the bus, maintaining his position by means of a leather strap attached to the bus body, the strap being held over his shoulder. The seats on the knife-board bus were reached by iron steps on the back, consequently it was not considered safe or proper for ladies to ride outside. The garden-seat bus to carry 26 passengers (12 in, 14 out) followed the knife-board, whilst at the same time there were bumper buses to give service to sparsely populated areas. The bumper bus carried inside passengers only and the means of boarding or alighting was controlled by the driver who released the door at the back by removing a strap from a peg by his dickey seat, the strap in question being fastened at its other end to the top of the door. Thus nobody could leave or enter without his knowledge. He was also responsible for collection of fares through a small trap in the roof. At first the control strap was passed across the front of the driver before it was anchored, thus his stomach was squeezed if a passenger attempted to leave without request. This led to a torrent of abuse from the driver to the discomfiture of the passenger and was soon discontinued to the relief of both.

The first motor-bus introduced by Tillings in 1904 carried a body specially designed to provide comfort for passengers and it formed a standard quickly followed by others. Prior to this there had been a few motor-buses of nondescript types, some single-deckers, others with a motor attached to a horse-bus body. I remember buses of the latter type with the driver perched high in the old dickey seat coming along to Tooting Broadway on Saturdays where they worked between that point and Mitcham. They belonged to the Star Company.

As might be expected the early motors had their teething troubles, no less the Daimler, Straker Squire and Dennis vehicles operated by Tillings, who evolved a kind of bastard bus in their Bull Yard works from the best parts of them. A good deal of expense was involved in keeping these buses up to road fitness, and a day and night staff of mechanics was maintained for this purpose. At this time it was the horse bus section that kept the motors going, but in a comparatively short time after the introduction of the petrol-electric vehicle the position was reversed and the full night staff of mechanics was dispensed with.

The first Tilling petrol-electric had electric motors between the side wheels driving each back wheel. It represented the combined efforts of Frost Smith, chief engineer of Tillings, Brown Bros. of Huddersfield, and Stevens, the electricians of Maidstone, thus it was known as the S. B. & S. type, but the men called it Queenie because it was so well behaved. There was no jerk in starting, the running was always smooth with little noise, the controls were simple and it was always reliable. It was said of them, with much truth, that the longer they ran the better they ran. Simplicity of control enabled displaced horse-bus drivers to pick up motor driving very quickly and being used to traffic they proved to be good reliable men. The first petrol-electric was slow in starting and it was difficult to work up to the permitted speed of 12 m.p.h. Nevertheless, there was a summons against a driver for travelling at 16 m.p.h. in St. George's Road, and despite expert evidence that it was practically impossible for this speed to be attained there was a conviction. Eventually the whole fleet was replaced by a modified speedier verson bearing the appropriate classification of TTA1. The bonnet sloped down to the front with the radiator behind it. Standing at Camberwell Green one day I heard a boy say to his mother, "Here comes one of those buses with a big nose." Later this model was altered somewhat to provide for increased seating capacity. This tendency to increase the number of seats finally meant the end of the petrol-electric fleet for it was difficult to build a larger bus and keep within the prescribed weight limit with this method of propulsion. AEC vehicles then became the standard Tilling fleet, but there were a few Straker Squires taken over from Timpsons, and the tail end of the petrol-electrics was when the London Passenger Transport Board absorbed them all in 1933. The writer saw an old Tilling petrol-electric bus three or four years ago at a fair on Peckham Rye where it generated lighting for all the shows in addition to moving goods or fittings from place to place—a real dual-purpose vehicle. None of the petrol-electrics was sent overseas in connection with the first world war but some of the men familiar with this type drove petrol-electric engines on the narrow gauge supply trains set up in France. An experimental petrol-electric tram ran for a time on the Tooley Street line but it was withdrawn because it was found the brakes were not good enough in damp weather, when the lines became greasy.

At a meeting at 55 Broadway, Westminster, comments were sought on the six-wheeled buses recently introduced. I ventured my opinion that the extra cost of this type would not be justified because the additional seats provided would only be occupied at the height of the peak periods. Furthermore the operating expenses would be higher on account of the extra parts and weight to say nothing of the upkeep of two extra tyres. All this was to the annoyance of a friend of mine who was strongly in favour of six-wheelers. Whether the opinion of a layman as opposed to that of an engineer was correct or not, the fact remains that when they came to the end of their useful life they were replaced by four-wheelers and this position obtains today.

Carrying out an inspection outside a No. 47 bus going through Bermondsey one summer's evening, I saw a boy run right in front of the bus to retrieve his ball. He was knocked down and the bus passed over him before it was brought to a standstill. To my surprise he came out at the back, picked himself up and ran off down a side street. I quickly followed, saying to the conductor in passing, "Get witnesses and wait for me." At the boy's house I persuaded his mother with some difficulty to come along with me to Guys Hospital bringing the boy for examination. There it was found the only ascertainable injuries were bruises on the right side of his head and his shoulder. He was discharged with a promise that he would be brought along immediately should any unusual symptoms appear. These did not arise, neither did any claim or blame reach the company. Buses then had a much greater road clearance than they have today, and there were two steps to the platform.

I wonder how many passengers travelling so swiftly over the Thames bridges in London today know that for a time in the early motor-bus days, buses were restricted to a speed of 4 m.p.h. when crossing the river. This followed an accident at Blackfriars Bridge when a motor-bus hit the parapet and narrowly escaped falling into the Thames. Not only did the companies have to suffer this reduced speed but also had to appoint Bridge Guards to see that it was carried out.

The last horse-bus was withdrawn from the Blackwall Tunnel route in 1912 and was replaced by motors with herringbone seats on top to enable the width to be narrowed there to avoid the risk of collision when buses passed in the restricted tunnel space. A narrow bus was operated at Brighton to serve the villages springing up in

One of the 80 Tilling STLs at Marble Arch in 1935. STL80(YY5380) was new in 1932, and had a Tilling 56-seat body. [*London Transport*

the valley of the Downs where the road width is small.

Harking back to the petrol-electric type, I must recount an incident at Loampit Hill, Lewisham. With a fully laden bus it was sometimes difficult to negotiate the hill successfully in the forward manner, and on such occasions it was the practice to run slowly down the hill to Shell Road, then turn and come up backwards, resuming the normal position at Tyrwhitt Road at the top. On one occasion a conductor who was not familiar with this manoeuvre shouted excitedly to the driver through the front ventilator, "We're slipping back; what shall we do?" "Do?" said the driver calmly, "better change the destination boards."

In the process of changing to the STL-type no restrictions were placed on our operations by the police authorities, but the General company were not allowed to work their vehicles over Richmond Bridge on account of its narrowness and restricted approach, nor on route 25 because of the sharp turn from Oxford Street into Bond Street. Tillings were not working on route 37 at that time and had never worked on route 25 but at the request of the General Company they operated an STL ("short type long") on both routes for several weeks without incident, and as a result the police removed their objections to the General operating STLs on these routes. Having helped the LGOC over their difficulty, we promptly had a charge submitted to us for the use of their Victoria stand, which was just as promptly paid, for these workings were outside the limit of our agreement and miles meant money to Tillings. There was a sequel to all this when the question arose whether the Victoria stand had any bearing on receipts, the outcome being that Tillings agreed the stand costs be included in the charges for road supervision, cashiers, tickets, etc., worked out on a mileage basis, for Tilling's receipts were adjusted to the level of the receipts per mile average for the whole of London.

A bus figured in an exciting incident at Tower Bridge when the bridge commenced to lift before all the traffic was clear, and the bus had to jump the gap. Route 78 has operated between Dulwich and Shoreditch for many years without variation because delays when Tower Bridge opens create an irregular service not suitable for extension. For the same reasons route 42 over the bridge is a comparatively short one.

Sir Geoffrey de Havilland in his pre-aeroplane days designed buses, but I have not heard of any of them being built.

It may be fitting, perhaps, to conclude my memories of vehicles and matters relating to them by telling a fine story. The early petrol-electric buses of Tillings had longitudinal seats inside with a grab rail along the roof on each side of the gangway to enable standing passengers to steady themselves. A lady entered a No. 36 bus at Kennington during the evening peak and stood at the far end of the gangway with her back to the fareboard. When the conductor approached for her fare she released her hold on the rail and opened her handbag, taking out her handkerchief to reach her purse. At that moment the bus swayed and in grabbing the rail she dropped her handkerchief which fell in the lap of a passenger who was dozing, apparently tired after a long day in the office. Presently the man awoke with a start, and following the direction of the eyes and head of the passenger next to him saw something white which he hurriedly tucked away inside his trousers, thinking he had not adjusted them properly. Needless to say, the lady did not seek the return of her handkerchief, but one wonders what the man's wife said when he was undressing and a lady's handkerchief fell out!

(From *H. Webb Recollects*)

Lord Egremont and the Phantom Motorbus

Atticus

As the third week of the Wilson Era dawns, a nostalgic backward glimpse of that dear, departed Macmillan's England. I have a pleasant little anecdote which, with its overtones of patrician whimsy and romantic ingenuity, already carries a period flavour. It could not happen to a technocrat.

The story is told by Jonathan Routh, the professional practical joker, who did those "Candid Camera" television programmes. It is his splendidly indiscreet contribution to the special "Granta Reveals All" issue of the Cambridge magazine.

According to Routh he was suddenly summoned to a lunch with the Prime Minister's Private Secretary, John Wyndham (now, as Lord Egremont, retired from Government service). His help was needed; no one else would do.

Routh was amazed. Mr. Wyndham was Harold Macmillan's closest confidant and friend. What Prime Ministerial crisis could this be? In fact, to this day Routh believes it was Mr. Macmillan's orders he was obeying. This, I understand on the highest authority, was not so. No matter, it was still real top level stuff.

The crisis was that Mr. Wyndham had, the previous night, undertaken a wager. At the time he lived in the Georgian purlieus of Cowley Street, right beside Parliament Square. He had, at a club dinner, bet his next door neighbour £50 that he could divert a London bus from its normal route, make it drive down Cowley Street (normally busless) and stop outside his house.

After considering the entire population of Great Britain Mr. Wyndham had decided that Mr. Routh and Colonel David Stirling (known as "The Phantom Major" for his daring commando raids) were the only men who could achieve this feat.

Instantly, over a delicious lunch, the three men set to work to plan the operation.

Could a double-decker squeeze down Cowley Street? Minions were detailed to measure and appraise, and came back to report that yes, with considerable backing and shunting at the bends, it could.

Could an ordinary scheduled service, a 3, a 59a, a 77, a 77a, a 156 or a 159, be lured off Millbank into the intricate back lanes of Westminster? The operations staff decided that using fake police would be cheating. Bribing an actual driver might lead to unfortunate repercussions.

This left two possible alternative methods. One, the long-term method would be to insinuate a conspirator into London Transport by having him hired in the normal way, and wait until he was screened, trained and actually driving one of the relevant routes (this method, it was decided, could take anything up to eight months to succeed).

The other would be to arrange for a fake inspector (Routh) to board the bus in Millbank, and for further conspirators swiftly to manipulate Road Up signs to divert the bus down Great Peter Street and into Cowley Street before either driver or passengers realised what was up. It was here, presumably, that Stirling's commando training, with its knife-edge timing and sense of ruthless discipline would come in useful.

By the end, the briefing plan ran to many tightly typed pages of foolscap. In its daring, scrupulous detail it made The Great Train Robbery look a slap-happy smash-and-grab. Once the bus had actually stopped in Cowley Street, Routh, as inspector, would inform the bewildered passengers that a typhoid epidemic had suddenly struck Westminster.

Emergency vaccination operations were taking place; so would the passengers please file out into the Casualty Clearing Station?

They would all then be ushered firmly into this thoroughly unclinical house where—as agreed in the terms of the original wager—the butler would be awaiting them with a silver tray, bearing a large glass of champagne for each passenger.

After they had been refreshed, and gradually disabused of any fears about typhoid, they would file back into the bus and continue their ride to Camden Town, King's Cross, Parliament Hill Fields, or

In Quotation Marks / 2

"The charabanc of the post-war period was a cumbersome monstrosity mounted high on a chassis which swayed dangerously on corners, and, owing to its solid tyres and inadequate springing, provided little in the way of comfort for its occupants."
[*Tramway and Railway World, 1930*

A few of the passengers on the left look as if they agree with the writer. Their transport is a 32hp Albion charabanc supplied in 1919 to Robert Taylor of Bannockburn.
[*R. L. Grieves collection*

"The first impression on getting inside was one of enormous length . . . It must be one of the smartest vehicles that ever plied for hire." (Contemporary newspaper report of the first run of London General ADC 6-wheeler LS1 in 1927) [*Photo: London Transport*

---

wherever. Wyndham also arranged for a fleet of hire cars to await in Lord North Street nearby, prepared to ferry any passengers who felt the prank had incommoded them.

John Wyndham next telephoned his neighbour? When, he asked, would it be convenient for the bus to arrive?

It was only then, in the cold light of some days after the original bet, that a warning note was sounded. Would there not possibly be more than merely risible connotations to this affair? Mr. Wyndham was so closely associated with the Prime Minister. Although there was no connection, mightn't some people assume there was? And mightn't some people not be amused?

Reluctantly, after much discussion, the project was abandoned. But Lord Egremont to this day considers that *morally* he won his fifty pounds.

If the new men at No. 10, Downing Street, give one half of the dedication, imagination and efficiency to their task as was devoted to the phantom bus there's nothing to fear.

(From *The Sunday Times,* November 1, 1964)

Day Out

K. C. Blacker

LEFT: A helping hand into the charabanc. RIGHT: Brighton 1920 and it's raining. Not really the day for a ride in a charabanc—even with the hood up.
[*Old Motor*

Wet again! A glimpse of rain-washed streets and mackintoshed passers-by, through the boarding house window spells gloom to even the stoutest-hearted holiday-maker, who picks at his egg and bacon without vigour, hoping that meanwhile the clouds will go. A dismal day lies ahead, looking in shop windows, visiting the pictures, drinking endless cups of tea and keeping well away from the drenched and dismal esplanade. Or maybe he will wrap-up his plastic mac for a few hours and take a coach excursion.

In 1920 he could not even do that. The coach of those days was very definitely a fine weather vehicle, May to September only. In fact it was seldom called a coach, the usual term being the picturesque but today outmoded "char-a-banc". Almost all were completely open and had the seats arranged in transverse benches seating five. Along the side was a row of doors, each giving access to one of these seats. There were usually hefty running boards. Most of these coaches were used on day or half-day excursions to or from holiday towns, and their owners developed as keen a weather sense as the owners of the "once round the lighthouse" boats. A season of bad weather often meant disaster.

When the Great War ended an enormous number of second-hand lorry chassis became obtainable at next-to-nothing prices and ex-servicemen and others invested in them. In the belief that the nation would become quickly char-a-banc conscious after wartime restrictions and would want to travel, suitable bodies were fitted and new char-a-bancs flocked on to the roads in large numbers. Business was brisk at first and there were not enough charas to go round. Unfortunately the severe trade slump proved a stumbling block as money became scarce; passengers became less numerous than was hoped and, alas, the weather was often far from kind. As may well be imagined, some owners with little or no motoring background struggled along with hopelessly inefficient businesses and did untold harm to others by reckless price cutting, before finally succumbing. Drivers were often indifferent or even downright

bad and many of the vehicles were unreliable and in bad repair. Some of the ex-military chassis had, in fact, been in doubtful condition when they entered civilian life. On the other hand the difficult times also nurtured a tough breed of busman who worked hard to overcome difficulty after difficulty, and who took a pride in his vehicle and good name. Many kept a lorry body as well as a char-a-banc body for each chassis, using each at the appropriate time, so as to employ their resources as efficiently as possible.

This was the coaching situation in 1920. The times were hard but it was an age of glamour in coaching that had not been seen earlier, and which will doubtless never return. Each journey was a challenge, for vehicles could often not be relied upon to return home without some sort of minor trouble, and the drivers had to be master mechanics and clever improvisers. They had also to be a tough race, prepared to set off on a day's jaunt in bright sunshine under a clear blue sky and to return home drenched and cold, and splattered with mud from other traffic. Roads were often well below present day standards, especially in the remoter areas like parts of Scotland and North Wales, and hills like Porlock and Countisbury meant a real struggle with crunchings of gears and clouds of steam.

Rivalry between drivers was keen, at times even fierce, and many were the races between them—followed, no doubt, by endless discussions over teas and wads of the respective merits of the solid Leyland, the speedy Reo and the silent Daimler, and reminiscences of the more outstanding battles. Drivers often appeared in court, although in fairness it should be recorded that most prosecutions were for speeding. The police in some areas seemed to keep up an endless vendetta against coaches travelling faster than the speed limit of twelve miles per hour, which became more and more ludicrous as the 'twenties wore on. Dangerous driving cases did exist, however, and at one time there was a very real fear in the industry that the increasing number of these would earn coaching a bad name.

Newspapers often reported cases of drivers hugging the crown of the road, dashing carelessly over crossroads and missing cyclists by a hair's breadth. Sometimes accidents were caused by tiredness, for coach drivers often had to work very long hours. An example in 1924 was Thomas Hargreaves of Wakefield who succeeded in sending six out of his eight passengers to hospital unconscious after knocking down a telegraph pole. He was fined £5 with £2 16s. costs and an endorsement for driving in his sleep. There was, of course, the devil-may-care brigade who were out for kicks and were far from tired. A case at Spilsby (also in 1924) resulted in a charabanc driver being fined £9 for preventing a motor car from passing, his second offence. He had taken the crown of the road to prevent an open two-seater from passing while his passengers stood up, jeered and shouted, and threw apples at the driver. This went on for about a mile by which time a queue of nine other cars had formed up behind the luckless victim.

Passengers could be something of a menace at times, and almost as much unfavourable comment reached the ears of the press about them as about their drivers. Works outings, football excursions and the like were very much the order of the day and parties of passengers found endless delight in leaning over the sides of the vehicles or throwing coins to children as they passed. A better class of clientele was sought by coach operators in increasing numbers, particularly as the working class of the day had little money to spend on pleasure. Coach travel at about 1¼d. a mile was not so very much cheaper than it is today (although it was even then cheaper than the railway) and so it became to some extent a medium for those who might like to have been described as middle, or lower-middle class. Much was done to encourage the better type of passenger; the emphasis was placed more and more on comfortable and luxurious vehicles. The 'finish' of many of the vehicles was excellent. A typical charabanc would have first quality buff leather, polished mahogany mouldings, spring cushions and squabs stuffed with the best hair, and a smart lino-covered floor. As time went by the charabanc went out in favour of the coach with its central gangway and 'torpedo' body. Numerous types of cape-cart hoods were tried to make coach travel an all-weather occupation, then side window frames—disappearing into the body side at first but more permanent later. So unpopular did the open charabanc become, in fact, that by 1925 coachbuilders like C. H. Roe of Leeds found themselves with large numbers of discarded bodies on their hands from chassis that had been re-fitted as all-weather coaches. The saloon coach with fixed top found a certain amount of popularity and there were numerous oddities. There was the Gotfredson "Sedan" which had a hard top but was laid out in charabanc style; there were bodies whose solid tops lifted off in one piece for fine weather work, bodies with roller shutter roofs, and real peculiarities like Strachan & Brown's de Dion with raised centre portion for extra visibility accommodating, below, a lavatory and a generous amount of luggage space. By the end of the 'twenties it had become clear that the only type of coach with a future was the saloon; occasionally with canvas head-centre, but normally with a sliding top.

Coach owners had to work hard to prosper, and were not slow to try new gimmicks. Long distance touring became more and more popular (sometimes paid for on the never-never) and hotels at holiday resorts all over the country became geared to dealing with the peculiar requirements of coach parties. Really daring and comparatively wealthy holidaymakers could venture by coach to the continent, and a

This poster for Scarborough was displayed in LNER stations in the 1920s. [*Old Motor*

few firms, like Chapman of Eastbourne, became very experienced in this particular field. Sometimes difficulties were encountered with local councils who were anti-coach and failed to realise the potential revenue they could obtain from coach parties, while others almost bent over backwards to attract them. Take, for instance, Bridlington, which in 1921 successfully negotiated with Leeds charabanc owners to run regularly to the town and where the local Business Men's Association arranged advertising and parking spaces, and compare it with the Bournemouth Town Council which, at the same time, was seeking to drive out the coaches by insisting that all vehicles carrying eighteen or more passengers should have two competent drivers. Proprietors sought to build up good will with their coaches and frequently adopted distinctive names or colours. Thus on the Llandudno sea-front, in 1922, you could see the Blues, the Reds, the Silvers, Creams and Purples, not to mention the Greys from nearby Colwyn Bay. Each had its colourful board advertising a trip to "The Switzerland of Wales" or perhaps "The New Alpine Tour" and its driver touting good-humouredly for custom.

Just as times were hard for coach companies, so they were equally difficult for the vehicle builders. The traditional, cumbersome, solid tyred British-built chassis were joined by small, pneumatic tyred foreigners which literally left them standing (despite the speed limit) and generally commanded higher fares. Many were American like the Federals, GMCs, Reos, Fords and Internationals, but some came from the continent, like the SPAs, Fiats and Lancias. The foreigners also inspired the six-cylinder engine, the drop-frame chassis (for smoother riding), and various other improvements, and did a good deal towards killing off certain British firms like Straker Squire, Palladium, Hallford and Durham Churchill. Some of the Britishers, like Guy, Burford and Dennis, answered well to the challenge but it was not really until the days of the Leyland Lion and the legendary Gilfords that British coach builders began to turn the tide.

Undoubtedly one of the greatest coaching events of the 'twenties was the introduction of regular daily long-distance coach services, starting with Greyhound Motors Bristol to London route in 1925, using 24-seat Strachan and Brown-bodied Dennis saloons, with special forty-five gallon tanks, to avoid refuelling en route. The express coach soon became quite the vogue and competition became intense on some of the "cream" runs. Some wonderful tales can probably still be told of spectacular speeds and wonderful duels on the Great

Some of the 40 charabancs that gathered in Guildhall Square, Plymouth in 1921, to take members of the Ancient Order of Foresters on a tour to Dartmoor.
[*Old Motor*

North Road route from London to Newcastle, where the Gilfords of Orange Brothers fought Galleys six-wheelers, Charltons Blues, Safety coaches, Glenton Friars and many others. Express Motors of Darlington started a sleeper service on this route late in 1928 and there then started a brief and financially unsuccessful craze in sleeper coaches culminating in Land Liners two impressive double-deck Guy six-wheelers on the London-Manchester run (30s. return including bed and breakfast).

By 1929 many of the coaches on our roads had attained a degree of comfort, and were worked with a standard of service undreamed of today. Compare the present day Bristol MWs on the London-Bristol run with Greyhounds four Associated Daimler 416s of 1927. These beautiful grey, dark red and black twenty-eight seaters had all that the coach traveller could wish, including a front saloon for twenty, a rear smoking compartment for eight and a small buffet in the centre. Comfort was the keynote in the red antique leather seats with headrests; you only had to pull a tab on the back of the seat in front and a small folding table, with glass top, was released, convenient for your lunch tray. Each seat had a bell for summoning the steward, and the individual roof lights were controllable by the passenger. The pile carpet was laid on felt, the footrests were carpet covered and, needless to say, there were heavy fringed curtains. All cabinet work was inlaid mahogany, and white lincrusta, embossed in dull gold, covered the ceiling. Naturally there was also a clock, a barometer, flower vases, an umbrella stand and a cigarette cabinet.

It is not surprising that, with enterprise like this, coaching not only turned the tide in the 'twenties but laid solid foundation for its future. What a pity so much of the character and originality has gone out of it today.

(From *Old Motor,* May 1964)

Country Conductor

R. L. Grieves

Most people will be familiar with the duties of the urban bus conductor, but things can be different in the country. In 1964 Robert Grieves spent the summer working with David MacBrayne Ltd. on their Glasgow-Tarbert route.

Last year I worked as a conductor for the well-known Scottish coach and steamer firm of David MacBrayne Ltd., Glasgow. MacBrayne has no double-deck vehicles, and as its services are very much different in character from those of most companies, readers might be interested to hear of a typical day's work of a conductor.

Although the firm operates many services throughout the western highlands and islands of Scotland, only two enter Glasgow, the company's headquarters. These are the Glasgow - Inveraray - Ardrishaig - Tarbert - Campbeltown service and the Glasgow - Glencoe - Ballachulish - Kinlochleven - Fort William - Inverness service. The latter operates through to Inverness in summer only. During the winter season it only operates as far as Fort William, leaving there on Saturday mornings and returning from Glasgow on Sunday evenings, allowing travellers the weekend in Glasgow.

I was attached to the Glasgow depot and usually worked the 09.00 departure from the city to Tarbert, a fishing village in Argyllshire exactly 99 miles away. Although the coach leaves at 09.00 from MacBrayne's own coach station in Parliamentary Road, Glasgow, the crews report up to an hour

An earlier MacBraynes conductor stands by his bus en route for Glasgow with a 1932 Park Royal bodied Maudslay ML6A. *[R. L. Grieves collection*

earlier depending on how busy the service is expected to be, in order to load the coaches. A large number of parcels and bundles of daily papers are brought to the station every day. These are for delivery by either of the two daily coaches to Argyllshire.

It is the conductor's duty to load these into the boot. This is not so easy as it may seem. There may be anything up to about 30 assorted parcels of all shapes, sizes and weights to be put off at various points en route, not forgetting the papers and, of course, the passengers' luggage. The 09.00 departure also carries the mail for delivery at four post offices along the road. On a busy Saturday morning in particular it is a real work of art packing the boot in such a way as to have everything at hand.

The boot has been packed, all the passengers are in their seats and the hands of my watch move towards 09.00 (in MacBrayne's it is the responsibility of the conductor to keep the bus to schedule). I check the £2 conductor's float, put it into my cash-bag and collect my box containing Setright 13405, waybill, ticket-rack and tickets. My driver for the day is Malcolm Campbell, one of the old hands with a lifetime of service driving buses.

"Cally," as he is affectionately known, knocks out his pipe and walks with me across to our bus. It is 52, the regular Tarbert service bus, a 41-seat Duple-bodied AEC Reliance. I close the front door behind me and we are off into the thick of the busy city traffic and heading along the Great Western Road towards Anniesland Cross. Although this is a long-distance service, it is still a stage carriage service and stops at any point to uplift passengers.

We are soon passing John Brown's shipyard in Clydebank, the home of the *Queen Mary* and *Queen Elizabeth* and the future home of the new Cunarder. We continue westwards along the north bank of the River Clyde and at Old Kilpatrick the railway and the Forth and Clyde Canal run alongside as well. This must surely be a point unique in Britain with four modes of transport running parallel—river, rail, canal and road.

As we are now unlikely to uplift any more passengers for a time, I make a start to take in the fares. It is a typical day in early summer and we have 25 passengers on board, this figure remaining fairly constant throughout most of the journey. The time taken to collect the fares varies according to the questions the passengers ask you. Particularly during the summer, many of the passengers are tourists who have a multitude of varied and sometimes rather involved queries which the conductor is expected to answer.

The passengers themselves can sometimes be difficult, but they must always be handled diplomatically. They are also often amusing, although they are usually oblivious to this fact themselves. I remember the "dear old lady" in fur coat with collar turned up on a sweltering day in August who was sure there was a draught coming from somewhere (almost everyone else in the bus had removed as much clothing as possible). "It's not so much for myself I'm worried, but Puss may catch a chill," she complained. Meanwhile, Puss, in a wicker basket on the seat beside the d.o.l. spat, hissed and scratched in a vain attempt to escape. There are more wild-cats left in Scotland than generally believed. I also recall the American lady who got quite excited when she caught a glimpse of the River Clyde as it widens just after Old Kilpatrick. She was sure that it was Loch Lomond and although I tried to tell her otherwise she remained quite unconvinced until we reached the genuine article.

The road along Loch Lomondside is narrow and twisting and as a large volume of traffic uses it, particularly in summertime, accidents are a frequent sight. For 16 miles our route borders the "bonny banks", often affording wonderful glimpses of some of the most beautiful scenery in Scotland. We leave Loch Lomond at Tarbet (not to be confused with Tarbert, our destination) and cut across the narrow isthmus to Arrochar at the head of Loch Long.

At 10.33 we draw up outside the village post office which, in common with most country post offices, sells a wide variety of general goods. I run round to the boot for Arrochar's mailbags and newspapers, carefully checking their labels as it is not the first time that the papers or the mail have been mixed up by a careless conductor and put off at the wrong village with chaotic results!

Shortly after leaving Arrochar the long climb is made up the "Rest and be Thankful" hill road. The old road, which is still used for motorcycle and car speed trials, can be seen winding up the hillside below us as we ascend.

After 10 minutes steady climb we reach the summit (700ft. above sea level). Already there and waiting our arrival is the 20-seat Bedford which works the 12-mile route down the twisting, single track road to the village of Lochgoilhead and then on to Carrick Castle, a scattering of houses on the edge of Loch Goil. The summit of the "Rest and be Thankful", or Lochgoilhead Road End as it is officially referred to in the MacBrayne timetable, must surely be one of the most unusual bus termini in Britain, albeit one of the most picturesque, as it is practically on a windswept mountain top.

We draw up alongside the "wee bus" in the layby and I go round the back of 52 to transfer the mails, parcels and papers while any passengers from Glasgow for Lochgoilhead or Carrick Castle change buses (this is a rare occurrence). Willie, the driver-conductor of the Carrick Castle bus, gives me a helping hand as usual, for there is a good deal to be loaded from 52 into the capacious compartment at the rear of 164. Usually, while we are stopped here, the bus which has left Campbeltown at 07.00 that morning for Glasgow draws up as well. Three buses at such a lonely spot is quite a sight.

At 10.50 we're off again and are soon bouncing over the switchback road from Butterbridge Farm into Cairndow. Good progress is being made to the new, level road being built slightly above us. Eleven o'clock and I'm once more round the back of the bus, this time for the mail for Cairndow Post Office. Cairndow is a delightful little village near the head of Loch Fyne. It is bypassed by the main road and is entered coming from Glasgow by a steep, winding single-track road.

At 11.20 we draw into Inveraray where we have a 15-min. halt. Inveraray Castle is the seat of the Duke of Argyll and is worth a visit, as is the small county town itself. Then we continue down Loch Fyne side through the pleasant villages of Furnace, Crarae, Minard and Lochgair. We are now nearing Lochgilphead and little groups of women gather at road ends and wait for us in order to do their shopping in the town. The bus is the meeting place for many folk

Driver Campbell (Cally) stands on the quay at Tarbert with MacBrayne 52, an AEC Reliance/Duple and 74, a Bedford VAS/Duple. [*R. L. Grieves*

who stay miles apart and the cheery chatter of housewives exchanging gossip both in English and Gaelic can be heard.

At 12.30 we arrive in Lochgilphead and the bus almost empties. I have several items to unload from the boot here. First, out come the all-important newspapers which are eagerly grabbed by a small crowd of schoolchildren who jostle every day for their arrival. I suspect these mischievous six-year-olds are treated to free sweets on their arrival at the newsagents. The passengers from Glasgow come round to collect their luggage and there are usually several local folk awaiting parcels from the city.

Only five minutes run from Lochgilphead lies Ardrishaig, turning point in summer for MacBrayne's steamer *Lochfyne* from Gourock. MacBrayne's also has a bus garage here. We stop at the pierhead outside the office where the connecting coach for Oban is waiting. After luggage and parcels are unloaded, we are away on the final lap of our journey to Tarbert. This stretch of road runs right along the edge of Loch Fyne for a good distance. The eight fare stages between Ardrishaig and Tarbert are mainly scattered cottages—Tigh-an-Rudh; Brenfield; Inverneill; Stronachullin; Artilligan Bridge; Erines; Meall Mhor; Stonefield.

Just after 13.00 we descend the hill into Tarbert. Below us lies the picturesque fishing village clustered round the bay with its tiny islands and the colourful yachts at anchor. We stop on the harbour, alongside which is usually gathered a number of the fishing fleet. Tarbert is, of course, the centre of the Loch Fyne herring industry. Who has not heard of a Loch Fyne kipper?

Awaiting our arrival on the harbour is the connecting bus for Campbeltown. This is operated by McConnachie of that town but MacBrayne's issue through tickets from Glasgow to Campbeltown which are valid for McConnachie's bus. Likewise, McConnachie issues through tickets from Campbeltown to Glasgow which are valid with MacBrayne. The usual exchange of newspapers, luggage and parcels is made with McConnachie's bus and then we move along to journey's end outside MacBrayne's small office at the end of the harbour.

At 14.15 it is time to attend to loading any luggage there may be into the boot ready for our 14.30 return to Glasgow. There is not much today, just two cases for Glasgow and a large crate of eggs for Inveraray Castle. 14.30 and we leave the pier at the same time as McConnachie's bus for its 40-mile trip down the peninsula of Kintyre to Campbeltown. For the last 44 years, McConnachie has operated between Tarbert and Campbeltown, holding the mail contract.

The return journey to Glasgow follows much the same pattern as the outward run in the morning, but with a few variations. At Lochgilphead the shoppers who came down with us in the morning return laden with messages.

At many cottages and road ends someone is waiting on our arrival in order to post their letters. A small postbox is fitted inside the bus near the door at the front. This box is emptied by a postman on our arrival in Glasgow. We leave Inveraray at 16.15 after a ten-minute halt. About 17.00 we wave to the crew of the afternoon departure from Glasgow for Campbeltown. Usually we pass as we are about halfway down the "Rest".

Back through Arrochar, Tarbet and down Loch Lomondside again. Passengers used to ask me if I ever got bored travelling up and down the same road every day. Personally, I fail to see how anyone could be bored, no matter how many times this road was traversed. At 18.40 we are back in the city centre after an easy run through the light evening traffic. Ten minutes later we pull into the coach station where 52 is fuelled and washed in readiness for the next day's run. I cash in the day's takings and mark out my time sheet. The work for the day is finished and I make my way home, already looking forward to tomorrow.

(From *Buses Illustrated*, September 1965)

Seeing Niagara —from a London Bus

Despite Americans' predilection for rapid transportation, the appearance of Leyland double-decker buses in Niagara Falls has been a resounding success. Tourists who at home favour the rushing taxi, or speeding commuter trains, seem to automatically turn to the picturesque double-deck buses. These buses, which arrived at Niagara Falls, Ontario, at the end of June 1965, and were put into service on July 1 are now becoming as photographed as the Falls Itself.

Taking a tour on one is to enjoy the sights of Niagara all over again but with a different perspective. Most amazing is the look on the faces of some of the pedestrian tourists when they see their first double-decker. The almost automatic look of amazement is followed by a mad scramble for their cameras. Visitors prefer the top deck, but the main novelty is the ride on a London bus.

The brainchild of Niagara Falls public relations man Cecil Farrell, it was carried through to its conclusion by an experienced tour operator, Norman Watson, who journeyed to England in early May and bought three retired units from London Transport. These had been selected with the aid of Leyland from those available and judged to be in the best condition. Any necessary spares are obtained and supplied by Leyland Motors (Canada) Ltd.

A private company, Double Deck Tours Ltd., was formed to operate the vehicles and they have been such a success that purchase of further vehicles has been decided upon.

The Niagara Parks Commission gave permission for the vehicles to operate within the boundaries of the Niagara Parks, a 35-mile long stretch of unparalleled beauty which runs alongside the world-famous Niagara River from Lake Erie to Lake Ontario and encompasses more than 3000 acres of sculptured and manicured gardens and lawns.

Double Deck Tours Ltd. hope the vehicles will be a reminder to visitors that the British reputation for quality of design and construction has not dimmed. Replicas of English sentry boxes, complete with imitation guardsmen outside, have been built as ticket booths. The fare for the round trip—which takes over three hours—is $3,50, and passengers may alight and rejoin en route.

(From *The Leyland Journal,* October 1965)

Where have all the buses gone?

In this age of planned and accelerated obsolescence it would seem logical to prophesy that within a few years, the British Isles will be slowly sinking under the weight of redundant buses. Not quite—but if you go to some of the islands off the West of Scotland, or to the Isle of Man, or to the Channel Islands, old buses litter the landscape, since there is no honourable retirement, and there are prohibitive ferry charges to get them back to the mainland. Meanwhile on the mainland, there are numerous contractors who are only too happy to lay their hands on well-maintained buses to carry their workers. And showmen, who clear out the seats to carry fairground equipment, and to tow their own caravans. And many a bus has formed the basis of a mobile grocer or fish-and-chip shop. Until recently there was a bus-turned-mobile hairdresser in East Kilbride. But then, it had been specially converted with a short back and sides.

One of the men who buy old buses is James Locke of Liberton, Edinburgh, who has received enquiries about second-hand buses from all over the world. An American who fancied an old bus to drive round New York as a double-deck status symbol, was only deterred when he was told of the £900 freight charge. Inspired, no doubt, by Cliff Richard, students often consider old buses for continental touring. A group of Cambridge students bought an old Scottish Omnibuses' AEC 'decker some years back, and covered many thousands of miles on continental roads, as did a Dundee party, who acquired an Alexander (Northern) Leyland for the same purpose.

Once Mr Locke sold a bus to a Spanish operator, and when he began to worry about his bill, the purchaser offered to pay him in oranges. Which would lead to some interesting speculation on rates of exchange.

Honourable retirement for one bus at least. This Wallasey Corporation Leyland now tours the country advertising New Brighton, disguised as the 'Royal Iris'.
[*R. L. Wilson*

This ex-Rochdale Corporation Leyland Titan TD5 with ECW body is now the North Western staff canteen at Lower Moseley Street coach station in Manchester. [*R. L. Wilson*

Now a fish and chip restaurant at Ingoldmells, near Skegness, this Bristol K5G with Park Royal body once saw service in the London Transport and Lincolnshire fleets. [*T. W. Moore*

By Motor Charabanc to John o' Groats

On Monday of last week a company numbering twenty-nine left Hope Street, Falkirk, comfortably seated in one of Mr. Alexander's handsome and well-appointed motor char-a-bancs en route to John O'Groats. Mr. Alexander himself was at the wheel. The first day's route was via Auchterarder, Perth Dunkeld, Pitlochry, Dalnaspidal, Dalwhinnie and Kingussie, where the party stayed overnight. Next day the journey was resumed to Inverness, and thence to Golspie, where the excursionists visited Dunrobin Castle and were allowed the privilege of going round the terraces and viewing the gardens. On the third day John O'Groats was reached by way of Wick. On reaching their destination the party had lunch at the hotel there and were photographed. On the way to John O'Groats the char-a-banc, being the first to visit this part of the country, created some little excitement in the countryside, the inhabitants of the various villages actually hiding in fear, much to the amusement of the occupants of the car. The return journey to Golspie was made the same day, and on the fourth day Inverness was reached via Dingwall and Strathpeffer. On the fifth day the return journey was continued via Nairn, Elgin and Forres to Huntly, where a visit was paid to the ruins of the Duke of Gordon's castle, and afterwards the party proceeded to Aberdeen. The sixth and last day's journey was made from Aberdeen, Stonehaven, Laurencekirk, Brechin and Forfar being visited, and on reaching Perth the company had tea in the Salutation Hotel. At this stage of the journey the company called upon ex-councillor Caw to preside over the gathering. Mr. Caw, in opening, said that they were reaching the last stages of the home journey, which, he had no doubt, would prove a most memorable trip. It reflected great credit on such a delightful tour. The whole journey had been made without a single hitch; the weather, with the exception of Thursday evening in Inverness, being of the finest. The company took this opportunity of presenting Mr. and Mrs. Alexander, as a token of their appreciation, with a solid silver set of tea knives. Mrs. Caw made the presentation in a neat speech and Mrs. Alexander suitably replied. The company then proceeded on the home journey, reaching Falkirk at 9 o'clock.

(From *The Falkirk Herald,* July 17, 1920)

The party rest at John O'Groats in their charabanc, a normal-control Leyland.
[*The Scottish Omnibus*

Buses in Miniature

Robin Hannay

Out of a total of 13 million motor vehicles licenced in this country, 79,000 are public service vehicles, which means that every 160th vehicle is (or should be) a bus. Yet the models made of buses in this country are very few and far between although there is obviously a need for them, as the bus is a feature of any town or main road scene. On model railway layouts there is usually a station, and passenger services are run with highly detailed locomotives and rolling stock. Yet when the modeller wishes to add to the realism with road vehicles, the buses available are usually very poor and not to a suitable or even accurate scale.

When a firm decides to produce one, inevitably, the London bus is chosen. In fact of seven examples introduced in recent years by five different firms, each produced one model of the Routemaster. Whilst agreeing the London bus is known throughout the world, and that toy makers have large export markets, the normal British double-decker is made in larger quantities than the Routemaster and is also exported in fairly large quantities to make it equally familiar to foreign eyes. At home there are very few towns or cities which do not have AEC Regents, Leyland Titans or Bristol Lodekkas providing the services. If one or even all three were modelled, they would have a much greater appeal than the Routemaster among both children and modellers. For the latter section of the market in particular, it is a great pity that a standard scale could not be agreed amongst the makers. As there is a large railway modelling fraternity who are customers for road transport vehicles, the '00' scale might well be adopted as standard. This gives a reasonable size to the model enabling a fair amount of detailing to be incorporated, without being too large or expensive, and would thus be acceptable to other collectors, and of course, to their main customers, children. The ideal could well be a plastic kit like the superb Airfix series.

The first firm to introduce a model of a bus was Meccano Ltd., who called their range 'Dinky Toys'. These were originally lineside accessories designed to complement their Hornby train sets, and included was a small model, about 2½ in. long, of the very advanced, and then (in 1934) newly introduced, AEC 'Q' type. This was a side-engined chassis with set-back front wheels and fitted with a centre-entrance double-deck body in the case of the Dinky model. Being to a scale of 125 : 1 it represented reasonably the outline of the original. It was joined by a tram, similar to the London E1 class made to a similar scale.

The first example to arrive to a larger scale was of a 'streamlined bus' which, without the windows, sold also as a van. It was about 3½ in. long, having a scale of roughly 1/95th. Whilst I think the van was the correct prototype and the bus an afterthought, it did bear a strong resemblance to a Dennis Ace built for Liverpool Airport in 1934.

Just before the war, a larger double-decker was made, and being to a scale of 1/78th it was close to the scale of the Hornby Dublo trains and suitable for background scenery. This was based on the London Transport STL class which had an AEC Regent chassis and LPTB body incorporating a roof number box. The external resemblance was fair and apart from the rear platform where could be seen what was supposed to be the staircase (the steps were only ¾ the scale size and finished about a scale 3ft. up making them a waste of effort) there was no internal detailing. When re-introduced after the war, the steps were omitted. Several post-war variants were made with the original body mounted on different types of 'chassis'. The first version had the radiator changed to represent the Guy Arab but after a few years, this was changed to a Leyland-style radiator and this was retained until the model was withdrawn around 1960. A version with the AEC radiator was also made in the 1950's.

A comparison of the famous old Dinky STL model and the current Routemaster. [*Meccano*

On all these models, the clumsy wings and crude headlamps of the original pre-war model were retained.

Dinky Toys turned their attention to single deckers after the war and produced several reasonably realistic examples. The first of these was based on the Guy Arab III chassis with a half-cab coach body similar to those built by Windover for North Western, but mounted on Leyland and Bristol chassis. This was to a similar scale to the double-decker, measuring about $4\frac{1}{2}$ in. overall. This was joined in August 1950 by a Maudslay Marathon 3 chassis on which was fitted one of the unusual and attractive observation coach bodies made by Whitson. The prototype seated 33 or 35 passengers and had a raised rear portion, underneath which was an extremely large luggage locker. The scale was similar to the half-cab coach which had by this time acquired a Leyland radiator. Early in 1951 a further coach was added to the ranks in the form of a fully-fronted coach bearing a resemblance to the Duple A series body of that time, with a Maudslay radiator.

With the advent of the underfloor-engined chassis, from the great number of bodybuilders who were in business in the early 1950s, Meccano chose to model the Duple Roadmaster 41-seat front-entrance coach body on a Leyland Royal Tiger chassis although all that could be seen of the 'chassis' were the wheels. Like the other single-deckers the body was simply a shell without any interior fittings. Exteriors were reasonably realistic but detailing was rather clumsy. Introduced in September 1952, the model cost 4s. 4d. and was roughly to '00' scale. At that time the full-fronted coach cost 3s. 6d. and the observation coach 3s. 11d. All these models continued in production until around 1960.

In 1956 BOAC was renewing its fleet of airport coaches throughout the world and had chosen the integral Commer-Harrington Contender. A model of this was added to the Dinky Toy range and, whilst still not having any internal details, it was finished in the BOAC livery of dark blue and white with the fleet name on the sides, and was quite attractive.

Around this time Exide batteries ordered a large quantity of the double-deck bus, which had the Leyland chassis by now, for publicity purposes. Painted bright red all over, it bore advertisements for Exide batteries on both sides and represented the final form of this veteran which, even Meccano realised, did not really look like the modern double deckers seen on the roads. Late in 1962 they announced a replacement in the form of a Leyland Atlantean rear-engined chassis carrying an MCW highbridge body, similar—though by no means identical—to vehicles currently entering service with both municipal and company operators throughout the country. For the first time interior details were included, taking the form of seats moulded in plastic, windows, and a driver. Externally there was an improvement in moulding. The results were of a higher standard than previously attained, with flashing indicators, destination apertures and a rear 'bustle' with the outline of the Leyland shield on it. Measuring just under 5 in. overall, it was approximately to '00' scale and cost 7s. 11d. Two versions were available, one finished in red with cream round the windows and roof, bearing a 'Ribble' fleetname, whilst the other had green in place of the red and had a mock crest in the middle of the words 'Corporation Transport'.

Models in the Dinky Toy range were intended to be used as background details on '00' scale layouts. After the war, a new series of models was started to a larger scale and these were known as Dinky Supertoys. However, it was not until 1964 that a British coach was included, and this was a twin steering three-axle Bedford VAL chassis carrying a Duple Vega Major 52-seat coach body. This had a large amount of internal and external detailing, including seats, windows, roof lights and flashing indicators. Provision was made for fitting a battery inside the body and when the vehicle was pushed along a curve the indicators would flash automatically. With an overall length of $9\frac{5}{8}$ in., it was approximately 1/45th full size. Most were produced in cream with a maroon flash applied by means of metallicised paper to give the effect of the chrome lining between colours. Finish was of a fair standard and an opening boot was incorporated. Original cost was 21s.

Although there have been developments in the British PSV industry in the intervening 4 years, no new Dinky Toy models have been introduced. Although the Atlantean is still fairly representative, the range does not include an example of a single-deck bus or coach. It is to be hoped that they will rectify this before long and that any new vehicles will be to '00' or 'HO' scale.

Lesney Products entered the toy market in 1953 with a model of the Queen's Coronation coach and following the success of this venture, introduced shortly afterwards their now world-famous Matchbox series. This reached a total of 75 different models and has remained at this figure with the older models being systematically replaced by newer versions. Included in the range are several buses. The idea of the range was to produce a low-priced toy to fit in a box of about the same size as a matchbox, which means that the models are to widely varying scales but they are all highly realistic.

First PSV to be introduced was inevitably an example of the then current London bus —the RT. It was about $2\frac{1}{2}$ in. long (about 150th scale) and whilst the body shape was good, the radiator and bonnet were unrealistic. The destination, I seem to remember, consisted of the number 5, which was the model number in the series. After a few years, this was replaced by the new Routemaster. Slightly longer at $2\frac{5}{8}$ in., the Routemaster body, radiator grille and bonnet were very well reproduced with correctly shaped destinations. The model was in a dark red livery with a silver grille and 'BP Visco-static' advertisements. In June 1965 this in turn was replaced by another example which was slightly larger, measuring $2\frac{3}{4}$ in. overall and being approximately 120 : 1 scale. This allowed more detailing to be included on the body—destination boxes, flashing indicators, lights, fuel tank cap and the latest grille introduced on RMF1254 —although this is a little foreshortened on the model. Internally, however, it is well-detailed, as a staircase, luggage space under the stairs and seats for 64 passengers plus a driver are moulded in white plastic. The bus is painted red and has 'BP Longlife' advertisements.

Two other London Transport vehicles were also included in the series. One was an example of the post-war MCW-bodied BUT three-axle trolleybus. Accompanying this was one of the well-known fleet of BEA airport coaches based on AEC Regal Mk. IV underfloor engined chassis with Park Royal observation coach bodies which incorporated a large luggage locker at the rear. Both were to a scale of roughly 150 : 1.

The first representative from the 'outside world' was a Bedford SB with Duple Vega 41-seat coach body. The scale was roughly 120 : 1 and like the others, but was simply a well-detailed die-cast shell with no interior detailing. All these models have been replaced—not, unfortunately, by other buses—and it was not until 1967 that a further bus was added. This was based on the Daimler Fleetline with Park Royal body that appeared at the 1966 Commercial Motor Show in Sheffield Corporation livery. It is well-detailed externally and, in line with the improvements that have been made to the other models in the Matchbox range in the intervening years, interior details are included. Moulded in white plastic, the seats and staircase are shown, whilst externally the bus is painted cream and carries advertisements on the upper-deck panels.

Following the success of the Matchbox series, Lesney introduced a smaller range totalling 16 models in all, which are replaced periodically. These were the famous 'Models of Yesteryear' and were to a larger scale than the Matchbox series and naturally more expensive, but included more detailing. Three passenger transport models have been included so far. The first of these was the famous 'Old Bill' bus. This was a 34-seat rear-entrance, open-top double-decker mounted on the normal-control B type chassis built for London General between 1912 and 1920. Whilst the interior seats were not included, seats were fitted upstairs and a driver with steering wheel was featured. Painted in red all over, the bus bore a 'General' fleetname and carried authentic advertisements and destinations.

The next new model, an LCC E1 class

tram, was to the same scale of 100 : 1. It was well-detailed externally, in London Transport livery with 'News of the World' adverts, but was devoid of interior fittings. A final addition was most interesting. It took the form of a horse bus pulled by two horses, and was complete with a driver. Seats were fitted upstairs, and it had a rear entrance.

All the Lesney models are to an extremely high standard of accuracy and realism, with new features being added all the time.

For their first bus model, Corgi Toys chose a coach of which there were only ten in existence. The reason for this was the publicity they received when Midland Red inaugurated a new era in travel in 1959 with the opening of the M1 Motorway. For motorway service Midland Red developed a special coach, the CM5, based on their home-made C5 touring coach. Powered by the BMMO 8.1 litre underfloor engine, the CM5s were specially geared to give a top speed of 80 mph, thus reducing the travelling time between Birmingham and London by half. The model was well-detailed inside and out, and chassis details were shown underneath. It was approximately to '00' scale.

The inevitable London double-decker—a Routemaster—arrived in 1965, at the same time as the Dinky Routemaster. Roughly matching '00' scale models, it was very similar to the Dinky vehicle, with a driver and conductress. The bonnet and grille were not accurately reproduced, and the destination boxes and the destinations displayed were not authentic. On the bright side, the interior had the correct number of seats—and even the outline of the Park Royal plate was included on the platform. It is a pity, though, to go to such lengths as this, and yet fall down as regards exterior detail. While the Corgi Routemaster is still in production, the Midland Red coach was discontinued some time ago.

Corgi's Routemaster model as originally introduced. [*Mettoy*

So far the models described have been small. An excellent example to a larger scale, 1/32nd, was introduced around 1963 by Airfix, in the form of a plastic kit to construct a model of the London General B-type bus. A high degree of accuracy is maintained throughout the 130 moulded parts, which include seats, clear plastic windows and even interior lights. The chassis is well-detailed, with chassis side-members, engine sump, remote gearbox and rear axle, front axle with tie bar, springs, gear lever, steering wheel, horn, lights, etc. Included are transfers of the 'General' fleetname and legal lettering and of contemporary adverts. Destination details for route 14 are also included, along with printed fare tables. Like all Airfix products, the B-type kit has detailed assembly instructions, and a good model can be made by even the most inexperienced modeller, provided care is taken.

Many of the LGOC B-type buses were commandeered to transport troops to France during the first world war, and Airfix introduced a khaki-painted version of the B-type kit in 1966, with card 'boarding' to cover the windows and upper deck. Unfortunately the standard is not as high as the original model.

This article does not profess to be an extensive review of all models that are or have been produced in this country, but is mainly an outline of the more popular ones. London buses figure largely among the ranks of die-cast models, and most toyshops have other plastic or metal toys, usually representing the RT or Routemaster types. Triang go one better with a moulded hollow plastic Routemaster about a foot high and twenty inches long, on which a child can sit, steering by means of a wheel mounted on the roof at the front.

Through the Lens

Everybody has their own views about bus photography. Some prefer straightforward 'record' shots of buses, others go in for unorthodox views. We asked six leading bus photographers to submit some of their favourite work, and one representative view was chosen from each selection.

R. L. Wilson sells large numbers of photographs to enthusiasts each year, so he prefers to concentrate on good record shots. Like many photographers, his first camera was a box Brownie, but he now uses a Canonette, a Kodak Retinette and a Zeiss Werra Mk I. For black-and-white work he uses Kodak Plus-X and Ilford FP3 film. The photo chosen shows an Ulsterbus Bedford SB/Duple coach (U176:2176MZ) meeting the "Caledonian Princess" at Larne.

R. L. Iles took this striking night view of an Eastern Scottish Bristol RE/Alexander coach at Barnsdale Bar on the overnight London-Edinburgh service. Richard Iles uses a folding Voigtlander camera, and Tri-X film.

Anthony Moyes uses an Agfa Silette Vario for his fine pictorial shots, usually with Ilford FP3 film. This superb rural view show Crosville Bristol LL6B SLB276 (NFM32) at Dawn, near Colwyn Bay.

D. G. Bowen specialises in photographs of Welsh buses, taken on a Zeiss Ikonette on FP3 film. This wintry view in Cardiff, shows Cardiff Corporation 3(EUH735), a 1950 AEC Regent III with Bruce body.

T.W. Moore is regarded by many enthusiasts as a master of bus photography. He has used a wide selection of cameras, from plate cameras through to 35mm cameras, and for this superb telephoto shot showing withdrawn buses in a Midland scrapyard, he used a Nikon F with a 350mm lens, on Tri-X film.

G. Coxon takes both record and scenic shots, and this view of a Bedford OB bus of Carruthers of New Abbey (9:KGN433) is an example of a good record shot. It was taken on a Ross Ensign camera, using FP3 film.

A Personal Portfolio

Gavin Booth selects three less orthodox views from his own photographic work, and explains why they are among his personal favourites.

Photography is a very personal thing. Like most bus photographers I take large numbers of straightforward record shots, but from time to time I like to try for more unusual shots. The Edinburgh Corporation Tiger Cub driving under a low bridge at Abbey-mount *(top left)* was one of a number of photographs taken when the roadway under the bridge was being lowered to permit double-deck operation on the busy 1 route. The Bedford SB/Duple coach *(above)*, Edinburgh Corporation again, was a late-evening into-the-sun shot in Charlotte Square, which catches much of the dignity of Edinburgh's New Town. The Leyland Royal Tiger coach *(left)* had just been presented to Greenlea Old People's Home in Edinburgh, and it seemed fitting to include two of the old people in my photograph.

"See Before you Buy"

R. H. G. Simpson, who regularly advertises "over 30,000 Bus, Railway Trolleybus and Traction Engine postcards", has been a full-time bus photographer for four years now, and each summer some 2,500 views are added to his collection. And as the selection increases, so does the demand from the enthusiasts who enjoy a photographic collection with the hard work of actually taking the photos.

As a teenager Mr Simpson started photographing trains in 1939. He widened his scope to include buses in 1944, and in the mid-1950s he started to sell a few postcards. Selling in quantity started in 1963, and the next year he went full-time.

Why do people collect bus photos? Primarily, Mr Simpson considers, to supplement those available in books. "There is also the fascination of collecting—like foreign stamps or antiques—and photos can turn up in the most unexpected places."

The range of photos is comprehensive, and Mr Simpson offers a good coverage of buses and locos that have been in service since 1939. Each summer Mr Simpson travels around Britain with his Rolleiflex T, which is fitted with a 16-exposure mask. New views are added as and when his printing capacity permits. "In practice this means perhaps 2,000-3,000 in the summer and 500 in the winter." Mr Simpson explained. "The problem is to give maximum coverage without letting the total become too excessive." Much of the summer is spent printing stocks of postcards in preparation for the coming winter.

Experience has taught Mr Simpson that straightforward record shots of buses sell best. Scenic photos are out. "Railway scenic shots sell quite well, but with buses, definitely NO!"

Whatever their preferences, Mr Simpson's "See Before You Buy" approval service allows enthusiasts to pick the views they really want. His best-selling views are express passenger steam engines and brand new buses, but all views sell eventually. "It's just a question of waiting longer for the right customer!"

Photographs of London buses sell very well—like this shot of ex-London Transport RTW489 (LLU979) in use as a mobile furniture showroom. [R.H.G. Simpson

When an operator is taken over, there is always a demand for photos. This view shows two buses of Moore of Kelvedon, a Guy Arab IV/Massey and a Guy Arab III/Strachans. [*R.H.G. Simpson*

One of Mr Simpson's best-selling views, a Crosville all-Leyland TD1, L115 (CK4222), which reached them via Ribble, Bristol and Wilts & Dorset. It was new in 1928. [*R.H.G. Simpson*

Wish you were here!

Old shops and ageing relatives are often the best hunting-grounds for picture post-card collectors. Buses figure in many street scenes, as shown by this small selection from the postcard collection of J.E. DUNABIN.

Buses are much in evidence in this elderly view of London's Marble Arch.

Market day at Bishop Auckland, with a fine selection of buses. The United Daimler CF6 on the right advertises "Travel by United to London. Return any day—fare 25/-."

ABOVE: Three David MacBrayne Maudslays meet the "King George V" at Fort William. BELOW: A Ribble Leyland/MCW Olympic waits at Bowness Bay, Lake Windermere, for the arrival of the "Swan".

Old Booth's Almanack

Gavin Booth's crystal ball makes some unusual predictions for the future.

JANUARY

Duples announce their 1970 coach designs. All models remain much the same, but with new mouldings and names. "We have to do this to keep up with Plaxton" they state.

Plaxton announce their 1970 coach designs. All models remain much the same, with new mouldings and names, except for the Panorama which reappears as the Panorama 70, all glass from the floor level up. "We have to do this to keep up with Duple," they state.

Suddenly Buses are IN. A Carnaby Street boutique does a roaring trade in old London Transport uniforms and second-hand ticket machines.

FEBRUARY

Derbyshire Police are investigating the overnight disappearance of the Tramway Museum at Crich. Foul play is suspected.

London Transport withdraws its first batch of Routemasters, which are sold to Birds at Stratford-on-Avon. A queue of Scottish independent busmen greets their arrival.

MARCH

Buses are IN. The Sunday Times *and* The Observer *each devote their Colour Magazines to them. The* Sunday Times *cover photograph features 42 Daimler Fleetlines spelling out "Omnimania" on the Yorkshire Moors.*

The Derbyshire CID releases the Omnibus Society Council after questioning in connection with the Crich disappearance. Identikit pictures are issued of a tramcar they wish to question.

Southdown order 50 Mercedes Benz 0302 coaches. Delivered in three days, but returned immediately on Government instructions. British manufacturers offer replacements "within two years".

APRIL

Following an incident in Coventry in which an alighting passenger inadvertently stepped on conductor Sidney Groin's toe, the Coventry depot of Midland Red comes out on strike.

Buses are IN. MGM make film version of latest Ian Allan ABC of London Transport Buses and Coaches, *starring The Beatles, Frank Sinatra and Sir Laurence Olivier.*

Duples announce their 1971 coach designs.

MAY

The entire Midland Red staff comes out on strike following the Coventry foot incident.

The search for Crich Tramway Museum switches to Dublin. "The search always switches to Dublin about this point," explains a police spokesman.

Buses are IN. Nova *features the Leyland spring collection—pastel-coloured Leopards, Panthers and Atlanteans posing in front of Twiggy.*

JUNE

Punch suddenly realises that all double-deck buses in cartoons should not look like London STLs. Instead they substitute roof-box RTs. A coach continues to be called a charabanc.

All company buses throughout Britain come to a standstill following the Midland Red foot incident. The Sunday Times *features photos of Sidney Groin's foot, taken by Lord Snowdon.*

JULY

Following the success of the 24-Hour Clock, the British Timetable Joint Working Party recommend the adoption of the 168-Hour Clock, covering the entire week. "This will avoid confusion between, say, 08.30 hrs on Monday and 08.30 hrs on Thursday. These will now become 32.30 hrs and 104.30 hrs."

Municipalities and independents support foot strike. Entire country at a standstill. Sidney Groin knighted.

AUGUST

Minister of Transport's offer of a 75% pay increase is accepted by foot strikers. Sir Sidney Groin elected to Parliament, and awarded the supreme accolade—asked to appear on David Frost TV show.

Severe summer. London Transport Red Arrow bus lost in 12-foot snowdrift at Hyde Park Corner.

Crich Tramway Museum is traced to a front garden in New York. Mr. Werner P. Trautbaum alleges he bought it from "a Mr. Steptoe".

SEPTEMBER

Western Welsh crews, faced with the appalling summer, are issued with special Survival Kits to combat the snow. These contain 2 tins Heinz Spaghetti; 1 Thermos of Mushroom Soup; 56 hot water bottles; 1 copy "Ian Allan ABC South Wales"; 1 pair wellington boots; 1 tin cocoa; 1 sledge; 1 set huskies.

OCTOBER

Sir Sidney Groin MP becomes Minister of Transport.

The August Bank Holiday (October 27) brings a 450-mile traffic jam from the Exeter by-pass to the outskirts of Edinburgh.

NOVEMBER

Investigating a serious shortage of buses which has resulted in drastic cuts affecting over 80% of London Transport routes, LTB discovers that 1,621 of their buses are touring the world, visiting various Trade Fairs.

Seddon announces that they have taken over British Leyland Motor Holdings. "This has come as quite a shock to us," states BLMH. "And to us," state Seddon shareholders.

DECEMBER

Plaxton announce their 1971 coach designs. Triplex shares soar.

Drivers Wild / 1

Red Daniells

Now why on earth would I need to signal? A 33B goes round this corner every seven minutes, and besides, it says on the back where we're going. We're a big organization, mate, so if you've got a complaint you get on to Head Office and see how far you get. Nowadays it seems us Transport workers are fair game for everyone. I don't make the rules. If I'm early I have to crawl to make up my time and if the road isn't wide enough for you to get past you go and complain to the proper authorities—not to me. They ought to close the towns to private traffic, anyway. And don't keep on about signals. When I'm pulling out into traffic I've got enough to do without indicating what should be obvious. Blimey, mate, I'm the biggest thing on the road and painted bright red—what more do you want?

(From *Drivers Wild*)

Preserving the Species

Prince Marshall

For the bus enthusiast, the ultimate goal would seem to be actually owning a bus. Many enthusiasts have in fact pursued their interest to this length, particularly in recent years. Prince Marshall, Managing Editor of "Old Motor", describes how he built up his own fleet of three buses.

The start of it all: ex-London Transport T31 photographed recently. This bus has changed hands three times since 1956 and is now well on the way to completion. [*Alan Cross*

It was a cold, wintry afternoon early in 1956—a Thursday afternoon at 4.30 p.m. to be precise—when the door opened and in walked a tall, big-boned, ginger-haired man, who limped down the short flight of stairs. In a cross between a Canadian and a Lancashire accent, he asked to look through some bus and tram pictures. Not an unusual request—for this was the Ian Allan Bookshop in Vauxhall Bridge Road, Victoria. The man's face seemed familiar, for I had seen him around at certain tramway meetings and we were on nodding terms.

The conversation got round to London buses. We quickly learned that we shared an enthusiasm for the same types of buses: the CR class (those little 20-seat, rear-engined experimental failures) and the ex-Thomas Tilling breed of ST class. By now, I had remembered my visitor's name. It was Warwick Jenkins. I told him how, back in 1953, I had actually tried to buy a CR to keep for preservation, but the price asked by London Transport was £250, then far beyond the reach of my pocket, and a few months after that, with Alan Cross—a noted enthusiast—and others, an attempt had been made to buy an old General bodied STL—STL 2674. That failed, too, for lack of money: we raised £93 of the £110 required.

Warwick and I talked a while on what vehicles were left of the old London fleet and how nice it would be to keep something which would always remind us of those years at the end and after the war, when there seemed to be so many interesting buses in London. Neither of us knew of any CR except the one kept by the Board and I knew of only one ex-Tilling ST, which languished in a scrapyard near Hitchin—totally beyond preservation. The only vehicle I could think of worth trying for was one of the old original 1929 T class, which was knocking about Chiswick Works for a few years. In fact, I was not sure if the Board still had it. By chance, I had a picture of a similar vehicle in my briefcase. With a gleam in his eye, Warwick said, "I see that bus every day. It passes the bank where I work in Chiswick High Road."

I didn't hear from Warwick any more until three or four weeks later when the Sister in the ward at the hospital where I was a patient came to me and said a Mr. Jenkins had phoned to say the price asked for the bus was £45. Well—that made me better right there and then!

It was August before we actually took delivery of the vehicle from the London Transport garage at Norbiton. One Sunday morning, the vehicle made its way through London to a small parking lot above Swiss Cottage Station. By this time, the vehicle had seven co-owners! We were all full of enthusiasm as to just what we would do with the vehicle. We would restore it back to what it was in 1929. Oh no, sorry, that was the source of a slight argument—as it was in 1945 (the entrance was not in the same position as it was when it was new in 1929). The weeks rolled by and we soon discovered that underneath the panels of our marvellous vehicle was nothing more than a lot of wet rot. That's when our first experience of bus preserving started in earnest.

With nothing more than a tarpaulin for protection, we worked evenings and week-ends in all weathers, snow or rain included, making all the progress possible, replacing the coachwork and panels, attempting to put it back to its 1929 condition—yes, the entrance went to the back!—and the argument was resolved.

In those months of 1957 and 1958, we bought another vehicle, a 1935 Gilford, which shared the space nearby T31. We must have given encouragement to many other small groups to think along the same lines of preserving a bus, for we kept hearing rumours that some one or some group was considering buying an old vehicle—usually one of those from among the literally dozens to be found on the island of Jersey. Our small group had formed itself into the Vintage Passenger Vehicle Society—the first society in the world dedicated to the preservation of ancient buses.

The Historic Commercial Vehicle Club, backed by great names in industry, gave us, in 1958, a sudden hope—a hope that we were not alone in the world and other people really did feel that these old machines were worth preserving. Perhaps a day would come when there would be a museum where we could ride on trams and old buses once again, a place where, fifty years hence, we could show what life was like when vehicles and pedestrians shared the same street level and just how crude—but fascinating!—these old machines are. Despite a few setbacks in those early days, the HCVC got off the ground, although not all those big names shared the untiring enthusiasm of the late Sir Henry Spurrier and since his death the club really has been on its own, without the support from industry we had hoped for.

In 1962, the HCVC ventured to put on a Run between London and Brighton. None of us in the club knew just how a venture of this kind would be received, so imagine how we all felt at the end of that day when we realised that the dignitaries of Brighton and the public had enjoyed themselves and were overwhelmed at the array of colour and interest that such a variety of old trucks, buses, steamers, taxis and the like had created. That Brighton Run was the first significant breakthrough. Now, every year, the Run gets bigger and bigger and there are more buses, trolleybuses and trams being preserved than we could ever have conceived.

One of the nicer things about pursuing our hobby is that only those who have enthusiasm bother to join our ranks, unlike many other activities where status might be the overriding factor. In fact, one has to have tremendous enthusiasm even to consider looking after a vehicle of such proportions: perhaps the kind of enthusiasm and staying power that went into the early days of the motor industry before the big financiers took over.

None of us really thought for one moment that bus preservation would ever take on to the extent that it has done. Whereas today a large number of people consider it fun to own an old bus, in those days we were looked upon as a little eccentric. In the same way, we never thought that the interest in old buses, by and large, would come from the younger generation—those not even old enough to remember the vehicles. In fact, it is very pleasing how young people today take a far greater interest in things of the past than any of our forefathers did. Perhaps it is because the older generation still remembers the days when every penny earned had to go towards the family budget and things like buses were nothing more than a tool in the process of earning a living. But more's the pity that the few enthusiasts and societies in existence in the 'thirties and forties' did not save from the boneyard some of the nicer early specimens.

T31 still has not been fully restored and in these ten years it has changed hands now for a third time. But other vehicles have been restored to a condition that even the manufacturers would be proud of if they were to deliver them as new vehicles.

My own fleet now consists of three London buses: a 1932 Wycombe-bodied 168OT Gilford (ex-Hillman Coaches of Romford), the ex-Thomas Tilling ST (yes, the one from the scrapyard at Hitchin) and a CR. The last-named came from the Board's collection when they found they were no longer in a position to look after it. Strange how events turn out.

I consider myself extremely lucky, but it is not luck that will keep these vehicles in the condition that we would all like to see them. It will mean sacrifice and plenty of hard work. You may well ask: is it worth it? Yes, a thousand times over. These ugly old beasts are a fine combination of machinery, coachcraft, shape and colour, pleasing to the eye. Whatever their shortcomings, they were creatures of character.

One of the London Transport CR class—"those little 20-seat, rear-engined experimental failures"—at Epsom in 1953. [*Alan Cross*

Saved for Posterity

A Pictorial selection of preserved vehicles

Michael Banfield's 'newest' old bus is ex-London General S454(XL8962), which was Concours runner-up at the 1968 HCVC Brighton Rally. The bus originally worked from Nunhead Lane garage, the site which is now the headquarters of Banfield Coaches. It was discovered in a deplorable condition in Berkshire in 1965 by the late Charles W. Banfield, who at one stage in his career was a LGOC driver at Nunhead Lane. [National Benzole

A group of members of the Northern Branch of the Omnibus Society unearthed this 1931 Dodge with 14-seat Robson body, some years ago in the village of Rookhope, in Weardale. VK5401 was originally supplied to Baty of Rookhope, and lay unused in his depot for over ten years. [J.F.Burns

This 1930 Leyland Lion LT1 (above) is one of the large fleet of preserved buses owned by the Lincolnshire Vintage Vehicle Society. It was new as Lancashire United Transport 202(TF818), and has a 30-seat Roe body. The LVVS rescued it from that one-time mine of old buses, Jersey, in 1959.
[National Benzole

When R.T. Coxon took this photograph of West Bromwich Corporation Dennis E/Dixon 32(EA4181) in 1939, he had no idea that he would be a member of the 32 Group, and involved in its restoration, a quarter of a century later. The lower photo shows 32 as it is today.
[R. T. Coxon

Another of Michael Banfield's superb vehicles. Jersey Motor Transport 25(J6332) was a 1932 Leyland Titan TD2 with 51-seat Leyland highbridge body. Banfield shipped it back to England in 1960, restored it to original condition, and from its first showing in 1963 it has won an enviable selection of prizes at various rallies.

The very first Bedford passenger chassis to be produced was this 1931 WHB with Waveney 14-seat body, supplied to Woodham of Melchbourne (TM9347). Mr. Woodham operated the bus until 1961, and it is now in the hands of the Arlington Motor Company, Bedford dealers. [*Arlington*

A recent addition to the ranks of preserved PSVs, ex-London Transport G351(HGC130), a 1945 Guy Arab with Park Royal body.
[*Alan B. Cross*

This former Exeter Corporation 1938 Leyland Tiger TS8 with 32-seat Craven body, 66(EFJ666) is only one of over 50 PSVs in the large West of England Transport Collection.

A typical Birmingham bus of the 1930s, 1937 Daimler COG5/MCW 1107(CVP207) was withdrawn from service in 1961, and bought by Barry Ware for preservation.
[Daimler

Cardiff Corporation bought 6 Crossley DD42/Alexander 53-seaters in 1949, and after 17 years service, 46(EB0900) was withdrawn in 1966 and bought by the Cardiff 46 Group for preservation.
[D. G. Bowen

Probably the best known collection of preserved buses is London Transport's own collection, presently on show in the Museum of British Transport in Clapham. Recent reorganisation has meant that several non-London PSVs in the Clapham collection have had to be resold, but London Transport have intimated that they intend to retain their own preserved vehicles in London in the event of the proposed transfer of many of the other exhibits to York.
Seven important London bus types are represented at Clapham. The oldest is the fully restored B340(LA9928), dating from before World War I. The others are K424(XC8059) of 1920, S742(XM7399 of 1923, NS1995(YR3844) of 1927, ST821(GK3192) of 1931, LT165(GK5323) of 1931 and T219 (GK5486) of 1931.
Until recently some of these vehicles could be seen participating in the annual London-Brighton Commercial Vehicle Rally, sponsored by National Benzole who kindly provided the photograph above showing K424 on the 1966 run. Overleaf Jan Condel gives her impressions of the museum at Clapham.

Rugs, Straw and Decency: Take an Omnibus / Jan Condel

On July 3, 1829, the cheapest coach fare from Paddington to the Bank of England was three shillings. The journey took three hours. The following day, the fare for a far speedier journey was only a shilling. That was the day George Shillibeer launched his 'new carriage on the Parisian mode for the conveyance of passengers'—and started London's bus service.

An exact replica of Shillibeer's omnibus heads the road section of the Museum of British Transport at Clapham. An apple-green paint job with floral wreaths decorating the body panels lightens the prophetically hearse-like structure, riding high on its crude elliptic springs.

Clapham Museum is a popular background for photographs of fashion models and recording groups. Here the Temperance Seven look suitably at home on the preserved K-type in the Museum.

The word Omnibus in large capitals on the vehicle's side was originally intended to be just a fleet name. Together with the driver's distinctive livery, it helped to make the vehicle recognisable to a vast illiterate population. Although the residents of still-peaceful Paddington resented it, Shillibeer's 22-seat omnibus soon took nearly £100 a week in fares. But in a time of tiny wages and incredible poverty his employees quickly learnt every trick in the book and the money turned in each night grew less and less. He tried installing an extremely costly meter, but with no success. The problem was only finally solved in 1893 when the London Road Car company started to issue every customer with a ticket from a bell punch.

As you can see if you wander along to Clapham for a fascinating two-bob's worth, the Shillibeer carried all its passengers inside. Three horses pulled the laden bus, which gives a fair idea of its massive dead-weight. By mid-century the number of people per horse had risen from eight to an average of 13.

Like so many pioneers, Shillibeer gained nothing. He insisted on running a route to compete with the brand new London/Greenwich railway in 1835 and eventually went bust. He turned undertaker, and that ensured that even his name was virtually forgotten. Although a few competitors had stolen his fleet name, Omnibus, a bus was still generally known as a Shillibeer. But who would talk of catching a Shillibeer to the Bank once sombre vehicles gold-lettered with 'Shillibeer's Funeral Carriages' became a common sight?

Standing beside that box-like pioneer in the museum, it's hard to realise the impact it has made. Hard, too, to think of the controversy it started. On its early runs, it was jeered at. Short-stage coach and cab drivers claimed that, according to the Stage Coach Act, it had no right to pick up and drop passengers in the streets. Such was the furore that early omnibus drivers were even known to chain themselves to their seats so that they couldn't be arrested.

At first, all passengers rode inside. By the early 1840s some of the mushrooming companies were providing a row of seats outside, behind the driver. At busy times, men even took to perching precariously on the rounded roofs. Yet when the first 'clerestory' bus, built for the Economic Conveyance Company, appeared in 1847 it proved unpopular with owners because the increased weight made it uneconomic. On this type of bus, the centre of the roof was raised to give inside passengers greater headroom and better ventilation, at the same time making a lengthwise bench on top at half price.

The Great Exhibition of 1851 brought an unprecedented boom to the transport world. Fares rose and the many companies who'd scorned the clerestory bus now nailed rough planks along their own roofs to make extra seats. These crude lash-ups resembled the felt-covered boards used in every Victorian kitchen for knife-cleaning, so that before long all buses with back-to-back seating were called knifeboards. Dozens of small firms sprang up, many to fail in the inevitable slump the following year.

One young upstart, though, was more successful than the rest. His name was Thomas Tilling, and his vintage 1851 knife-board stands behind Shillibeer's omnibus in the museum. Tilling's first route, using a four-horse omnibus known as The Times, was between Peckham and the West End. Speed and punctuality were his keys. His was the fastest omnibus on the route. It started on time and ignored all the public houses that lined its road. Intent on efficiency, Thomas Tilling was the first bus owner to refuse to make a round tour to pick up passengers.

Early buses, like early trains, mainly served the middle classes. The poor were far too poor to go where they couldn't walk. In their quest for custom, owners would provide services that would make the most PR-oriented transport manager smile in 1966. For example, newspapers and periodicals were commonly provided for passengers. One Mr. Cloud tried furnishing his buses with books, but passengers killed the service by taking away half-read volumes. Tilling introduced the first monthly season ticket and included a reserved seat and a rug in his fee for regulars.

Yet all was not jet-liner luxury. There was always the odd pirate company which would undercut its rivals' fares, then hold its passengers to ransom on some lonely common. Crack drivers would race a rival regardless of the passengers' or public safety. Accidents were frequent and so were hold-ups. Even in the centre of towns, road surfaces were bad and springing on the buses was minimal. With few exceptions, there were no brakes until the 70s—although hand-applied skids helped the horses on long descents. Till 1853, the insides were unlit at night. Afterwards a single dim and smoky oil lamp on the door as often as not fulfilled the letter of the law. And it wasn't until 1899 that an LCC order required buses to carry a light outside.

Simple iron rungs and later a ladder led to the roof. Stairs were not introduced until 1881, long after the 1867 law requiring buses to stop only on the left hand side of the road did away with the need for a centre rear door. Most confusing of all for strangers: it was impossible to tell just where a bus was going. Regulars recognised the livery but the routes were only shown in general terms, destination boards were unheard of, and there were no route numbers.

Public transport was a competitive business, and even the biggest companies worked on tiny profit margins that precluded gambles. Weight simply couldn't be increased because the horses were already working to their absolute limit—which is presumably why the staircase was so long coming. And anyway, there were restrictions, then as now, on the size of omnibuses allowed into the centre of London.

Keen-eyed visitors to Clapham will notice that the Tilling knifeboard bus of 1851—a really wonderful relic, original paint and all—has an outside stair as well as the 'decency boards' first fitted a decade later. The bus on show was used until 1895 and modified as time went by. The original ladder was removed in the '80s and replaced with the new staircase. The decency boards along the side were fitted at much the same time, so that 'A female might with propriety and ease ascend to the roof seat.'

The year 1861 saw the formation of the London Road Car Company. Its first three buses were knifeboards, but with access by a front staircase. Later in the year it introduced an even bigger improvement—the first garden-seat omnibus. Although the idea of having pairs of forward facing slatted seats had been in use on the continent for 30 years, it had been a long time coming to England. The buses were still open, straw was still spread on the floor in winter to help keep passengers' feet warm, wheels were still iron shod, but the bus as we know it today had begun to take shape. The LGOC's garden-seat bus of 1895 in the museum proves that.

Rubber tyres were a big problem with the relatively heavy omnibus. As early as 1894 a newspaper was extolling the virtues of the products of the Pneumatic Tyre Company, shortly to be fitted experimentally to one of Tilling's buses. In fact sheer cost put even solid rubber tyres right out till 10 years later. In 1902 a set of these tyres for a one ton vehicle cost 10d. a mile to run. Even after 1904, when the first tyre mileage contract was signed at 3.0576d. a mile, one operator was complaining that his tyres ripped from their rims after 200 miles.

The first years of this century were anxious ones for bus owners. They had vast amounts of money invested in horses, stabling and vehicles. A country-wide complex of small breeders, buyers, fodder suppliers, auctioneers and finally knackers relied largely on the horsedrawn bus for its livelihood. Body design had reached a peak of lightness and strength. Passenger demand was rising yearly. In 1905, LGOC's fleet reached 1,420 buses in daily use, and there were over 17,000 horses in the company's London stables. Yet to keep customers from their direct competitors and also from the railways and tubes, owners suddenly had to find money to replace their entire fleet with motor vehicles, their stables with garages, grooms with mechanics, and to retrain their horse drivers. And all this for a largely unknown and unreliable public fad. . . .

At first, anything so long as it was horseless would do. Steam, electric, petrol electric and internal combustion engines all had their followers. Once started, the changeover was rapid. The last regular horsebus in London ran in August 1914. Ironically, the Kaiser war made the task easier. Men and horses went to the front. At home, shortage caused a boom. Profits rose for the first time for years. Then the buses themselves were requisitioned. And sure enough there on the museum floor, standing proud as a Chelsea Pensioner, is one of the LGOC's B-type buses so famous in old war photographs. Altogether, nearly 3,000 of this successful series were built between 1910 and 1926, and well over 1,000 served overseas. This particular bus is very much in working order. It leaves the museum for the funeral of any Old Contemptible and, last year, was driven round London selling poppies.

The return to peace brought new competition among bus-owners. Pirate operators sprang up again. Some were one-man, one-bus setups with romantic names recalling stage-coach days. There were the Tallyho, the Victory and the Lion as well as the Uneedus and Havaride.

As engines became more reliable, restrictions eased. In 1925, the LGOC's NS (Nulli Secundus — second to none) appeared. It was the first bus with a roof and with pneumatic tyres. In 1928 the speed limit for buses with pneumatic tyres was raised from 12mph to 20mph, and again to 30mph in 1930. In 1929 the police prohibition on windscreens or any form of cab was removed.

The NS is familiar to many people, so it comes as a shock to see some of the many school-age visitors to the museum stop and laugh at the beetle browline as they rush around filling in their I-spy sheets. They finish the bus section in front of a 1923 chassis, scouring the caption boards to find out when the first Tilling-Stevens petrol electric bus was introduced. Only a few of them realise the direct connection between this and the primitive knifeboard bus emblazoned in faded gold with the name, style and title of Thomas Tilling, Jobmaster.

(From *Car*, September 1966)

Two of the fine London buses preserved in the Museum at Clapham, the superbly restored B340 (above) and K424. [Gavin Booth

'Vintage' buses of the 1990s

Gavin Booth

Motoring writers frequently resort to predicting which of today's family cars will achieve immortality and, of more interest to the average motorist, which will retain their value in the years to come. If we are to believe them, then Standard Vanguards, Jaguar XK120s, Triumph Mayflowers and Jowett Javelins will be taking their places in the historic car rallies of the 1990s.

With buses such predictions are more difficult. Mass-production methods in the motor industry have meant that while one Daimler Sovereign car may look very like another, a Daimler Fleetline bus for Birmingham Corporation will look quite different from a mechanically similar Fleetline for Leeds Corporation. British bus operators value their individuality so much that enthusiasts of the future are going to find it increasingly difficult to select really representative buses for preservation.

When the first flush of preservation spread over the country, many relatively old buses were still in service—or at least were known about. This was in the late 1950s, and there were still many pre-war buses in service, mainly as a direct result of the enforced slowing-up of new vehicle deliveries during the war years. Many excellent specimens were saved from the breakers hammers at this time, but the supply must be nearing exhaustion. Claims have probably been staked on the few remaining old buses still in reasonable condition, and while there must still be vintage buses lurking in dingy sheds, most enthusiasts have turned their attention to newer buses. Sometimes this produces the odd situation where a "preserved" bus may in fact be newer than similar vehicles in service in the same part of the country, but then preservation is very much an individual thing, and enthusiasts are more concerned with their own tastes than with the overall preservation pattern. Because of this Leylands and AECs tend to outnumber the products of the other major chassis builders in the lists of preserved PSVs.

What is likely to be preserved in the future? Again individual tastes will play a

LEFT: An Alexander (Midland) Albion Viking VK43L with Alexander Y-type body would be a fitting representative to preserve in the future. The author boards a 1967 example in Cumbernauld new town. RIGHT: Two notable designs produced for the big company groups, the Bristol/ ECW LS (TOP), exemplified by a 1955 Southern National example, seen at Camelford, and the Marshall version of the BET bus style is seen on a 1964 Ribble Leyland Leopard, at Hawick.
[The Scottish Omnibus; KW Swallow; Gavin Booth

great part in such decisions, but there are certain vehicles that deserve to remain for future enthusiasts to see, largely through their significance when they were new.

Living in the largest centre of population in Britain, Londoners have made sure that London Transport vehicles will not be forgotten. In addition to London Transport's excellent collection, many more recent London buses are in private hands, and it looks as if this trend will continue, and we shall eventually see RFs, Routemasters and even Red Arrows among the ranks of preserved vehicles. Outside London, the greatest degree of standardisation can be found in the Tilling and Scottish fleets, and to a lesser degree in the former BET Group fleets. A Bristol-ECW Lodekka 60-seater of the mid-1950s merits preservation for the important part this design has played, and the Bristol-ECW LS of the same period is another candidate. The ECW bus and coach bodies produced for the LS were notably good examples of functional design, but the later designs for the Bristol MW chassis lacked much of the subtlety. The BET group have a long tradition of specially-designed bodies, although contracts were placed with several different bodybuilders, all of whom were expected to produce largely similar bodies to the BET specification. The best examples of standard BET bodies are probably those on 36-foot chassis fitted with curved front and rear screens, a development of the previous, rather uninspired design. This design has proved so successful that many independent and municipal operators are specifying it on new deliveries, and it has inspired other bodybuilders to produce basically similar styles. Ideally, if a BET-style 36-foot bus is to be preserved, then it should be a vehicle ordered for a BET company, say a Northern General or Western Welsh Leyland Leopard. The BET Group also influenced double-deck design—although to a lesser degree. The MCW Orion body, which has been in production for over 15 years, was developed jointly by MCW and BET engineers, and the Leyland Atlantean chassis is another

example of close manufacturer-operator co-operation. As far as coaches are concerned, BET companies have tended to choose established designs, often going through phases of favouring one particular coachbuilder. The success of the Harrington Cavalier design was due in some measure to the orders placed by BET firms, and as the Cavalier surely deserves a place in the ranks of preserved vehicles, it would be fitting if the body were mounted on a Ribble or Southdown Leopard.

The Scottish Bus Group has always pursued a varied vehicle policy, but their association with Alexanders, the Falkirk coachbuilders, has produced some individual styles. For a while Alexander bodies could rarely be found outside Scotland, but English and Welsh operators started to specify Alexander bodies, and, after many years of functional, if traditional, designs, Alexanders were prompted to produce more exciting styles, like the popular Y-type single-decker and the 'Glasgow' style double-deck design for rear-engined double-deckers. If eventually a Y-type is preserved, then an Albion Viking from one of the Alexander fleets would be a fitting example. Over 400 Atlanteans with Glasgow style bodies are actually in service in Glasgow, so one of these vehicles would seem eligible. Although this body design has been copied by other builders, the original Alexander styling is still the most successful.

Municipalities have always valued their individuality—almost to the point where one wonders if they are just being different for the sake of being different. With the advent of rear-engined double-deckers, the larger municipal operators went back to the old practice of evolving 'special' bodies to their own specification, but in the late 1940s/early 1950s large batches of similar vehicles were placed in service in different areas. It would be good to see a preserved composite Roe-bodied double-decker, possibly a Leeds AEC Regent or Northampton Daimler CVG6, and a Faringdon-style all-Leyland PD2. The Roe and Leyland designs are both unusual in that they are almost universally popular among bus enthusiasts, something which rarely happens.

LEFT: A traditional-style Roe composite body, mounted on a Huddersfield Daimler CVG6LX-30 RIGHT: Operating in another hilly centre, an Edinburgh Corporation Leyland PD2/20 with MCW 'Orion' bodywork. [*Daimler; Gavin Booth*

In recent years independent coach operators have tended to restrict their orders to a small group of specialist builders. As small orders are generally involved, a Bedford/Duple for 'X' will differ very little from a Bedford/Duple for 'Y'. Yet for some reason independent coaches seem to have little attraction for the preservationist, and coaches are badly represented among preserved vehicles. For purely historical reasons, it would be interesting to see one of the flamboyant and ungainly underfloor-engined coaches that enjoyed a brief popularity in the early 1950s, often with bodies by builders who did not last until the end of the decade. Similarly it would be appropriate to preserve an early Bedford SB/Duple—a significant design—yet it appears that, as long as a type of vehicle can be seen on the streets, there is no panic to acquire one.

What else should be preserved? This is largely a question of individual tastes, and is open to discussion, but these are some of the vehicles which could well be running down to Brighton on HCVC rallies in the next ten or twenty years: a Midland Red S6; a Western Welsh Leyland Tiger Cub/Weymann; a MacBrayne Bedford/Duple mailbus; a Ribble Tiger Cub/Saro; an Eastern Scottish AEC-Park Royal Monocoach. Some significant coaches: a Burlingham Seagull body, perhaps on Daimler Freeline chassis; a Sheffield United 36-foot AEC Reliance/Plaxton; a Bedford VAL with Duple Vega Major body; perhaps a coach with a Yeates Riviera body, to remind us how much coach design has improved in ten years. Double-deckers are more difficult: some "local" products would be significant, like a Manchester Corporation Crossley DD42, a Wolverhampton Guy Arab or an Aldershot & District Dennis Loline. Other possibilities: a Liverpool Atlantean; an Edinburgh Leyland PD2/MCW Orion; a West Riding Guy Wulfrunian; a Midland Red D9; a Western SMT Albion Lowlander. There are undoubtedly many more candidates, but it will be interesting to see how many of these predictions are borne out.

Following the Leader

In 1965 London Transport was awarded one of the Royal Society of Arts' Presidential Medals for Design Management: it was one of the two organisations honoured for long pioneering in the field. These two articles trace different aspects of London Transport's design policies. In "Pioneering Policies" Corin Hughes-Stanton, Editor of "Design", sets their current policies against their background of growth from independent, unco-ordinated beginnings, and briefly discusses the problems London Transport will be facing as it designs for the future. In "A Poster Tradition" Harold F. Hutchison, Publicity Officer to London Transport, describes how Frank Pick and his successors have fostered the high standard of poster art that is well known today.

Pioneering Policies

Corin Hughes-Stanton

London Transport had many births and, although it has been unified since 1933, much of its present character and quality stem directly from its multiple beginnings.

In 1907 the London Passenger Transport Conference was established (with Sir George Gibb as its chairman) to introduce a measure of co-operation between the different railway companies. This conference decided to use the "UNDERGROUND" symbol (designer unknown) on all its stations. The bull's eye sign (designer also unknown) was the symbol of the independent London General Omnibus Co., and the two symbols were not finally amalgamated until six years later in 1913. Although symbols are now the stock in trade of every graphic designer, this circle bisected by a horizontal line (adapted for station names

TOP LEFT: London Transport's famous RT design—"the largest and most highly standardised group of buses in the world". LOWER LEFT: A normal-length Routemaster in Park Lane. [London Transport and route signs) remains one of the best symbols ever devised in modern times.

In the same year Sir George Gibb, who was chairman of the District Railway and deputy chairman of the Underground group, appointed Albert Stanley (later Lord Ashfield) to be general manager of railways in the Underground group. It was Lord Ashfield who created a unified transport system out of a collection of rival and conflicting companies. In 1910 he became managing director of the Underground group of companies, and then chairman of the London Passenger Transport Board when it was established in 1933. The period before and after the first war was mainly one of electrification and amalgamations. Even so, when the LPTB was set up it took under its wing over 170 railway, bus, coach train and trolleybus undertakings. The board's policy from the start was to standardise design.

Many types of buses were taken over, but except for the coaches serving the Green Line routes most of them have been double-deckers. Standard models were introduced as soon as possible. The most important was the RT. Designed just before the second world war under the direction of Eric Ottaway and A. A. M. Durrant, then chief engineer (buses and coaches), it forms the largest and most highly standardised group of buses in the world (it was not, however, put into quantity production until 1945). It is a logical, highly efficient design, 7ft. 6in. wide and 26ft. long, and seating 56 passengers. Mr. Durrant, as chief mechanical engineer (road services) then led the design and development of the RM (Routemaster) bus which began service in 1959, and on which Douglas Scott collaborated.

Meanwhile, between 1933 and 1949 the Underground spread out from its centre network to Cockfosters, High Barnet, Epping and West Ruislip, serving and encouraging the spreading dormitory population. As with the buses, so with the railways. The rolling stock was brilliantly designed and continuously improved upon by a design team led by W. S. Graff-Baker.

But this development meant not only building new stations, but also modernising old ones. This too was superbly done, and the man who created those aspects of the system which the public notice most was Frank Pick. An administrator, he was perhaps the twentieth century equivalent of a Medici. He had joined the Underground group in 1906 and as commercial manager he saw that "to assemble artists and architects round such a vast business enterprise would be to bring Morris's ideals up to date". In 1915—in the middle of a devastating war—he commissioned Edward Johnston to design a new type face. It created a revolution in British lettering, and even today there is no likelihood of its being superseded on London Transport. In 1933 Pick became vice-chairman of the LPTB and commissioned Charles Holden to design uncompromising stations. Through Holden's design for the LPTB's Broadway headquarters, Frank Pick became an early and controversial patron of Epstein, Eric Gill and Henry Moore.

But the designs being carried out within London Transport were equally important. Christian Barman was made responsible for the visual impact of the transport system. The detailing of moquettes, tiles, station seats, fare boards, ticket machines and bus shelters, as well as of the buses and trains themselves, all have a directness and fitness for purpose that have probably never been achieved before or since on such a large scale.

Lord Ashfield and Frank Pick have been criticised for being more interested in graphics than in transport planning, and are charged with contributing towards the subtopian sprawl around London. This is not really true. They were not asked to plan a transport pattern. They were asked to meet and satisfy a transport demand. But in meeting this demand with the finest standards of design and quality, they have enabled London Transport to satisfy a far larger share of the commuter traffic than might otherwise have been the case. Many urban transport systems are designed for the least well off and look like it. Lord Ashfield's great achievement was to produce a one-class transport system which is respectable as well as being handsome, clean and efficient. As a result the bowler hats have been as loyal to London Transport as have the cloth caps. This gave London an almost unique breathing space in which to plan for its foreseeable traffic problems. That the opportunity has not been taken is not the fault of London Transport.

The key to the success of London Transport's design policy is extremely simple. It is to appoint the best possible men to head various departments, and then to expect them in their turn to appoint the best staff that can be found, ensuring all the time that design is part and parcel of every piece of equipment. London Transport design has always been functional: it has never been applied. This was the policy of Lord Ashfield, and it is still the policy today.

Frank Pick was one of the results of this policy. He is the best known, but he was not an isolated figure. W. S. Graff-Baker, until a few years ago the chief mechanical engineer (railway services), was not only a great engineer but also a brilliant administrator.

The London Transport Board is small and compact: it has four full-time members and three part-time members. To it report the heads of 23 departments. These are divided into four main groups, each under one of the four full-time board members. London Transport also has a Design Panel, set up in 1963 by Sir Alec Valentine. The chairman is Eric Ottaway, and the rest of the panel is composed of the architect, the publicity officer and the design consultant.

The reason for the creation of the Design Panel was to produce new thinking. On the operating side the original design incentive came from Frank Pick. While the tradition has continued, the risk of the policy's running down became obvious. London Transport has recently moved into a period of new technology, and will soon be buying a lot of new equipment. The danger which faced the board was that inspiration might peter out and that design ideas conceived 25 years ago would get grafted, not necessarily suitably, on to the new equipment.

The Design Panel is not an executive body, nor does it discuss policy questions. Problems like the number of seats in a bus are not its concern. Nor does it report formally to the board. Its job is to question the projects put to it, and when necessary suggest possible improvements. The proposals for new equipment, large and small, are discussed by the panel with the operating managers and anyone else who might be involved in their use. In these discussions of the aesthetics and shape of the new equipment, the aim is to ensure that the necessary compromise between mechanical requirements and design of ergonomic needs is the best rather than the easiest.

Mr. Ottaway believes very strongly that design should not be superimposed. The board expects the creative aspects of new designs to come from the people on the job, be they engineers, doctors or graphic designers. Mr. Ottaway says, "We never do anything for appearances's sake which will in any way detract from functional needs or efficiency". Built into all specifications are only those materials, processes and shapes which are the most efficient.

Because London Transport has to live with what it designs, it cannot play with fashion or design premature obsolescence into its equipment. Although it no longer manufactures its buses and trains, both chief mechanical engineers have development sections which design rolling stock to take account of regular, fundamental overhauls. The reason is that while the manufacturers make the vehicles once, London Transport has to rebuild them many times.

Industrial designers are called in to help when specialist work is needed. For instance Professor Misha Black, besides being on the Design Panel, is also design consultant for the Victoria Line, working with the chief mechanical engineer on the rolling stock and with the architect on the stations.

The effect of the Design Panel and the far reaching developments introduced by various departments cannot be fully assessed until the Victoria Line is completed. But the projects which come into operation from 1967 onwards (and which are likely to affect the whole of the London Transport complex) started life during the period when it seemed that London Transport was hardly progressing at all.

London Transport, which has a long record of finely engineered buses, is not just sitting back now that it has its Routemaster buses. Although the number of people using buses in London has declined by 30 per cent during the last 10 years, buses are likely to have an increasingly important role to play during the next decade. Therefore the development division is working on prototype designs for three possible new buses: a new Green Line coach, a front-loading pay-the-driver bus, and a standee bus.

But design, be it engineering or graphics, cannot exist in isolation. To be effective each detail must be a rational response to a wider design concept. Ultimately London Transport will only hold its own through the design of things like the improvement of interchange facilities between rail, tube and buses, the introduction of a new Central London tube and the extension of the Bakerloo and Victoria lines.

Naturally, many planning ideas which need urgent consideration—such as bus-only lanes on throughways—cannot be decided by London Transport alone. But, as Anthony Bull, a member of the board, recently said, "It is not possible to separate the provision of transport facilities from the use to which land is put; land use and transport act and react on each other".

The significance of Sir Alec Valentine's chairmanship of the London Transport Board has been his initiation and support of a new design policy, coupled with his success in making the public realise, in the short time since 1959, that it is necessary to have a properly co-ordinated and rationally planned public transport system. The new chairman, Maurice Holmes, has the very considerable task of creating such a system. The degree to which a good design management policy is valid will depend on the success of London Transport in this wider area of design.

(From *Design,* May 1965)

A good example of the fine posters specially designed for London Transport: "Green Thought" by E. R. Bartelt, 1961. [*London Transport*

A Poster Tradition

Harold F. Hutchison

Any attempt to see in the right perspective these fifty years of art in the service of the public must first pay tribute to Frank Pick. He came to London in 1906 from the North, where he had qualified as a solicitor and had first whetted his appetite for transport work on the old North Eastern Railway. By the time he died (in 1941 at the age of sixty-three) he had become Vice-Chairman of the London Passenger Transport Board with a reputation both in the world of transport and the world of art which links him with the enlightened if despotic art-patrons of the Renaissance. In both the shrewdness and the idealism of Frank Pick lies the best answer to those critics who may still think that good wine needs no bush.

It was Frank Pick who first thought it a good thing for a station to have front windows—illuminated invitations to sample the attractions on sale within. Infinite pains are taken to ensure that the invitations are both arresting and tempting, with a colourful challenge which is never braked by information better given inside, when invitations have been accepted and the public has arrived. The quality of appeal which achieves this has to be matched by a quality of efficiency, speed, convenience, comfort and beauty—a standard of service—to make the whole system worthy of the greatest of cities.

London Transport treasures a tradition which is applied to every side of its activity. 'Fitness for Purpose' there must be, but alone it is not enough; a new idiom has been created by and for London Transport, and Design is its commonest proper noun.

But, in paying tribute to an idiom directly inherited from Frank Pick, respect is due in almost equal measure to the artists who have translated that idiom into poster art. Most of the distinguished names in British graphic design have been added to the index of those who have thought London Transport worthy of their skill, and some of those names have first achieved distinction by posters done for London Transport. The traditional picture-postcard view had at all costs to be avoided. If so hackneyed a subject as Windsor were required, it needed a Clive Gardiner or a John Farleigh to see it afresh. When the Wembley Empire Exhibition was in all men's minds, it was Fred Taylor (whose graceful span bridges nearly the whole period) who applied his architectural imagination to a bird's-eye view and produced a remarkable synthesis of Westminster and Whitehall. If simple days-out can attract more traffic, then let so rare a fancy as Betty Swanwick's or John Burningham's make sport of simplicity and create a new technique of poster beauty. Let a Kauffer or an Unger express the essence of a river, wood or theatre in colour combinations that none but they ever saw, and the ordinary man will soon find himself tempted to enjoy it all in his own way. To such artists, to those scores of others whose work has contributed to the whole panorama of its publicity, London Transport expresses grateful thanks; because in following the Pick tradition we have created a reserve of public goodwill which is beyond price. The most efficient of transport organisations must sometimes fail because of the human element or the weather or the waywardness of machines or all three of them; it is at such times, when performance is less than perfect, that the system needs the goodwill of its passengers most. In this sense good poster art takes its place with all the other evidences of thoughtful management in persuading the customer that the business is properly run.

But the justification of the London Transport idiom is not only in terms of economics: a public service should have a social purpose. A station must be a shelter where you catch a train, but it should also be a contribution to the oldest of the arts —architecture. Posters can be stuck on walls and turn architecture into huckstering; they can also be works of art framed as mural decorations proportionate to the whole façade. London Transport believes that it is wise publicity to give the public what it wants in such a way that it feels it to be more than a want—something better that soon becomes a need; and the severest critics of any new poster are those who now feel affronted when they think that London Transport is providing something less than the very best. In the definition of 'best' there will always be opportunity for dispute, and although London Transport is famed for the courageous way it has aesthetically shocked some of its public, it nevertheless has always kept its feet firmly on the ground. For every startling innovation by a genius there are half a dozen easily accepted paintings by more conventional artists—and the discovery of genius is subject to the laws of supply as well as to the laws of demand. The conventional in art need not be undistinguished, and if the standard is set sufficiently high, genius may sometimes emerge. This idiom by which we are constantly trying to reconcile the ideal with the practical—as old a problem as the Roman 'honestas' and 'utilitas'—has no fixed formulae. If design in all things great and small is the key, then design must keep pace with technical progress, and with changing art-moods and modes. As new stations can be built, or old ones can be renovated, they will be to new patterns but to standards not less exacting than the old. As new buses and trains are designed, they will express contemporary fashion while they adhere to principles of design which are beyond the whim of fashion.

Since the last war, new formulae have been developed which are still in the old tradition—for example, the same standards which have always applied to the pictorial content of a poster are now applied to the text. The artist is given scope, sometimes unimpeded by any text whatsoever, to please even those who run. The man of letters—the copywriter—can deliver a message finely expressed and beautifully presented for those who have time to stop and read. Both art and language are fluid —the new formula can provide for progress in both; and, in due course, it will be superseded by some other formula to fit the mood of tomorrow. Meanwhile, today's contributions can be measured against this conspectus of the past—they will sometimes suffer from the comparison, but the effort to equal the past, and sometimes to surpass it, will go on. . . . To please all the people all the time is impossible, that is why London Transport's posters are so varied—some will appeal to special tastes, some will appeal to all, some will shock the many, some will disappoint the few.

(From *London Transport Posters*)

A Matter of Design

Gavin Booth

The design of buses and coaches is now becoming a matter for closer co-operation between the bodybuilders and the operators. Some of the most successful recent body designs have been the direct result of such liaisons, which seems to emphasise the complacency that exists in certain of the large body-building firms, who otherwise would be quite content to produce what in some cases are 10 to 15-year-old designs. Just as operators are showing a greater interest in the appearance of their vehicles, there is a growing public awareness of design. The similarity between some bus bodies produced by "rival" builders is in a few cases blatant imitation, but is more often the result of similar thinking in the development stages. This happened in the private car world when in 1966 the Ford Cortina, Hillman Hunter and Vauxhall Viva were announced within a few weeks of each other, all looking suspiciously alike. Each development team had a conception of what-the-public-wants, and it turned out that they each had a similar conception.

Even for the builders, awareness of the importance of bus design came fairly late. In the early days buses owed a lot to tramcar design, and were straightforward, functional vehicles. Internally the "furnishings" were simple and basic, externally they were intricately painted, lined and lettered. The first **real** buses appeared in the mid-1920s, vehicles that were actually designed for the purpose, rather than simply adapted from goods vehicles. Chassis were designed for passenger-carrying, and instead of the high-framed lorry chassis they were used to, passengers had only to surmount a couple of steps to gangway level. From the outside looks remained square and functional, but bus transport was enough of a novelty in the early days, and enjoyed such popularity in the 1920s that operators had little bother attracting passengers.

The advance in body design went hand-in-hand with the advance in chassis design. When the manufacturers started producing

'Design' at its most basic. A rugged-looking Maudslay, one of the original fleet bought in 1906 to start the Scottish Motor Traction company. [*Scottish Omnibuses*

more refined chassis, the coachbuilders were given greater scope, and, encouraged by the operators, who now appreciated the importance of design in a highly competitive industry, they produced many notable styles. Some were outrageous, some were simple and effective, some were complete failures—yet every design played its part in the evolution of bus and coach styling, which reached an unprecedented peak by the mid-1930s. The introduction of more stringent regulations governing vehicle construction, with the 1930 Road Traffic Act, was another important factor.

Following the 1930 Act the company bus groups we know today expanded greatly, often by acquiring smaller operators who could not last the pace. Already the main groups, the Tilling companies, the BET Federation and the SMT group, were evolving standard buses for their own use. Tilling used the manufacturing sides of two associated companies, Bristol and Eastern Counties; the BET designed their own bodies; the SMT used bodies built by the coachbuilding side of Alexanders, which at that time were available only to associated companies. Alexander bodies were the only 'restricted' products, and Bristol/Eastern Counties vehicles, and BET-designed bodies were available generally. There were no restrictions the other way, as with the Tilling group between 1948 and 1965, and companies in all three groups bought a wide variety of vehicle types.

Single-deck buses in the mid-1930s were still basically simple and functional-looking vehicles. Chassis like the side-engined AEC Q of 1932 and the Maudslay SF40 of 1935 allowed designers a short-lived field day with full fronts, but advances were subtle and undramatic.

Advances in coach design were more obvious. From the open charabancs and early canvas-roofed vehicles of the 1920s, the increase in long-distance coach travel, coupled with the need to compete with the fast streamlined express trains of the railway companies, forced coachbuilders to revise their ideas. At first coach bodies were based on bus shells, suitably refined with external mouldings and interior decoration, but soon definite 'coach' shapes started to appear. At a time when the railway companies and car manufacturers were discovering streamlining, the coachbuilders kept face by producing some quite remarkable coach bodies, often one-off jobs for Motor Shows, that were never repeated. It was also a time for gimmickry, and sleeper coaches, radio coaches and observation coaches appeared on the roads. Some coaches had kitchens, some had toilets—there was even a coach with a

Two years makes all the difference. Contrast the Leeds Corporation AEC Regent/Roe exhibited at the 1935 Commercial Show (ABOVE), with the fine Leeds AEC Regent/Roe exhibited in 1937 (RIGHT). [*Roe*

piano at the 1929 Motor Show. But most of these novelties were fairly short-lived, and more emphasis was placed on passenger comfort, resulting in plushly finished interiors, with quilted roofs, veneered wood facings and discreetly curtained windows.

The Leyland Titan TD1 of 1927 introduced a whole new concept in double-deck bus design, and the AEC Regent of 1929 took it an important stage farther, producing a basic pattern which has not really changed, even now, for the 'traditional' front-engined / rear-entrance double-decker. Double-deck styling had a fling in the 1930s, with streamlined and fully-fronted styles, which, if they were none too successful, did contribute something towards cleaner lines. Towards the end of the 1930s some significant designs appeared. At the 1937 Motor Show Roe exhibited an AEC Regent for Leeds Corporation, with 4-bay window layout which foreshadowed many designs of 10-15 years later. In 1938 Leyland introduced a modified version of their standard double-deck body, that was probably one of the most aesthetically pleasing designs of all time. After the second world war this style was reintroduced, and the basic body remained in production until Leyland stopped building bus bodies, in 1953. Probably the most significant design of the time was the London Transport RT, of which 150 were supplied in 1939/1940, and which could be regarded as the prototype of the standard double-decker of the late 1940s/early 1950s.

During the war years all new design ideas were stillborn. Certain bodybuilders were authorised to produce bodies to a rigid wartime specification which made no concessions to comfort. Towards the end of the war these standards were relaxed, and for a while after the war some builders continued building buses to wartime designs, to aid production. Others resumed postwar production with bodies based on their last prewar designs, and it was not until about 1950 that really *new* designs reappeared.

The widespread acceptance of underfloor-engined single-deckers at this time allowed designers to broaden their scope, and although many of the first underfloor buses were remarkably box-like, the first underfloor coaches were quite different. Like some grand reaction to the restrictions of the 1940s, big, brassy, flamboyant coaches took the road in their hundreds, but after this first flush of freedom the designers quietened down.

General coach styling seems to have come the full circle. After a period of over-decoration and widespread use of curved

ABOVE: The early 1950s were noted for flamboyant coaches. The Windover body was one of the better examples. This AEC Regal IV/Windover 32-seater was supplied to Blue Bird of Hull (NAT359)
RIGHT: A good example of operator/coachbuilder liaison, the. MCW bodied Atlanteans supplied to Liverpool Corporation.
[K.W. Swallow; Gavin Booth

window-lines, coaches are now reappearing with simpler, straighter lines, and with ornamentation largely confined to the front, where large chromed grilles—often with little practical purpose—are presently in vogue. The Duple Commander and Plaxton Panorama designs, with well-chromed fronts and large areas of glass, are typical of the current trend, and the simple side mouldings allow operators to apply their own particular livery schemes ad lib. Consequently Xs Plaxton-bodied Bedford can look quite different from Ys Plaxton-bodied Bedford, and a basically sound design can often be ruined by an ill-conceived colour scheme.

When the first rear-engined double-deckers came on to the market in 1958, it was disappointing to discover that the leading bodybuilders had done little else than vary their existing designs. The initiative to produce new designs came from operators like Glasgow and Liverpool Corporations who approached coachbuilders and developed their own styles. Other operators have now followed this lead.

PSVs must, of necessity, be fairly box-shaped, but some of the early designs on underfloor chassis carried this idea rather far. Happily there has been a trend in recent years to introduce more shape into purely functional designs, and curved windscreens have played their part in convincing builders that even a functional service bus need not necessarily look plain and unexciting.

British car design in 1968 owes much to the Americans, and much to the other car-producing European nations, who have evolved "international" styles with no real national characteristics. Bus and coach design is quite different. British coaches bear little similarity to European coaches, which in turn bear little similarity to American coaches—which is maybe just as well. The continentals have always led the way in coach styling, and many of their better ideas have tended to rub off on British designers. On the other hand, the two markets are very different, and the British coachbuilders have been to the fore in developing such refinements as larger side windows and better ventilation systems.

There are those who firmly believe that the basic concept of the bus as a functional, utilitarian vehicle demands the simplest box-like shapes, with the minimum of extraneous decoration. Conversely there are transport executives who consider design before comfort, and who produce buses with impossibly high window levels, badly-angled staircases or restricting seats. Somewhere in the middle are the operators and manufacturers who produce the best buses.

LEFT: Typical of good modern coach production, a Leyland Leopard PSU3 with Duple Commander III body, supplied to Grey-Green. ABOVE: The clean and inviting interior of a Black and White Daimler Roadliner with Plaxton Panorama body. [*Leyland; Plaxton*

A Transport of Delight

Michael Flanders and Donald Swann

One of the very few songs about buses. "A Transport of Delight" was composed by Michael Flanders and Donald Swann for their show "At the Drop of a Hat".

Some talk of a Lagonda, some like a smart MG
Or for Bonnie Army Lorry, they'd lay them down and dee
Such means of locomotion, seem rather dull to us
The Driver and Conductor of a London omnibus
Hold very tight please *(ting, ting)*. Hold very tight please *(ting, ting)*.

When you are lost in London and you don't know where you are
You'll hear my voice a'calling "Pass further down the car"
And very soon you'll find yourself inside the terminus
In a London Transport, diesel-engined, 97 horse-power omnibus.

Along the Queen's great highway I drive my merry load
At twenty miles per hour—in the middle of the road,
We like to drive in convoys, we're most gregarious
The big six-wheeler, scarlet-painted, London Transport, diesel-engined, 97 horse-power omnibus.

Earth has not anything to show more fair
Mind the stairs *(mind the stairs)*, Mind the stairs *(mind the stairs)*,
Earth has not anything to show more fair
Any more fares *(any more fares)*, Any more fares *(any more fares)*.

When cabbies try to pass me before they overtakes,
I sticks me flippin' 'and out as I jams on all me brakes,
Them jackal taxi-drivers can only swear and cuss
Behind that monarch of the road, observer of the Highway Code, that big six-wheeler, scarlet-painted, London Transport, diesel-engined, 97 horse-power omnibus.

I stops when I'm requested, although it spoils the ride
So we can shout "Get out of it—we're full right up inside!"
We don't ask much for wages, we only want fair shares,
So cut down all the stages—and stick up all the fares!

If tickets cost a pound a piece, why should you make a fuss?
It's worth it just to ride inside that thirty foot long by ten foot wide,
inside that monarch of the road, observer of the Highway Code,
that big six-wheeler, scarlet-painted, London Transport, diesel-engined,
97 horse-power *(97 horse-power)* omnibus.
Hold very tight please! *(ting, ting)*.

The Sting in the Tail

A selection of rear-engined buses and coaches

One of Daimler's prototype Roadliner SRC6 chassis, CWK641C with 49-seat Duple body, used as a demonstrator.
[Colour plates by courtesy of Jaguar Cars Ltd

A Glasgow Corporation Leyland Panther with two-door Alexander body. This bus was exhibited at the 1964 Commercial Motor Show.
[Photo by Gavin Booth; Colour plates by courtesy of The Leyland Journal

ABOVE, LEFT: An Eastern Scottish Bristol RELH with Alexander coach body, on tour in the Trossachs.
[Photo by Allan Boath; Colour plates by courtesy of Travel Press

ABOVE, RIGHT: Leyland's Atlantean is represented by this BOAC example with 54-seat body, seen in Chelsea.
[Colour plates by Courtesy of The *Leyland Journal.*

LEFT: Western SMT operate a large fleet of Daimler Fleetlines, including six of these 33ft examples with 83-seat Northern Counties bodies. One is seen at Abbotsinch Airport.
[Photo by Gavin Booth; Colour plates by courtesy of the Transport Holding Company

It's quicker by Bus

Kingsley Amis

Jim Dixon had just received a message that Christine was catching the one-fifty train, and wanted to see him before she left. Although Christine 'belonged' to Bertrand Welch, Dixon planned to change all that.

'I'd better get moving, then,' Dixon said, making calculations.

'You had. I'll tell the bag you won't be wanting your lunch. Go and get on that bus.' Atkinson lowered his face towards the paper.

Dixon ran out into the street. He felt as if he'd been hurrying all his life. Why wasn't she getting a train from the city station? There was an excellent one to London at three-twenty, he knew. What was her news? At any rate, he had some for her; two lots, in fact. Did her unexpected departure mean that she and Bertrand had had another row? A bus was due to turn up College Road between one-ten and one-fifteen. It was that now. The next was at one thirty-five or so. Hopeless. He ran faster. No, she wouldn't have left just because of a row. He'd stake anything on her not being the type to take a revenge of that sort for a thing of that sort. Oh, hell, her news was probably just that 'Uncle Julius' was going to offer him a job. She wouldn't have counted on his having heard so quickly. Would she have asked him to come all this way just to tell him that? Or was it all just an excuse for seeing him again? But why should she want to do that?

He suddenly bounded aside into the road, where, some yards away, a large taxi-like car was waiting in a side-street to insert itself in the further stream of traffic. Dixon cut through the nearer stream, bawling 'Taxi, Taxi.' Just what he wanted. In a moment he was able to make for the far pavement, but the taxi simultaneously drove out into the main road and began to gather speed away from him. 'Taxi. Taxi.' He was nearly there when the face of the Principal's wife, wearing a hat like a biretta, appeared at the back window, frowning at him from what had looked like an empty rear compartment. The taxi was clearly not a taxi, but the Principal's car. Was the Principal in it too? Dixon veered away through an open gate into someone's front garden, where he knelt for a minute behind the hedge. Was it really so important for him to meet Christine at the station? Wouldn't he be able to get in touch with her afterwards through 'Uncle Julius'? Had he still got the piece of paper with her phone number on it?

"The conductor watched him immobile from the platform".

A rapping on glass made him turn round. An old lady and a big parrot were glaring at him from a ground-floor window. He bowed deeply, then remembered his bus and ran out on to the pavement. A couple of hundred yards away a bus was coming slowly up the hill from the city. It was too far off for him to be able to read its destination screen, and in any case his exertions had misted his glasses over. But it must be the one and he must get it. He sensed, as far as he could sense anything at the moment, that something would go badly wrong if he failed to turn up at the station, that something he wanted would be withdrawn. He began running even faster, so that people began to skip out of his way and look at him with wondering resentment. The bus, unable for the moment to begin its turn into College Road, was halted in mid-traffic and was, he could now see, his bus. He ran steadily towards the corner of College Road, but the bus began moving again and reached it before him. When he next saw the bus it was halted about fifty yards away up College Road, and someone had just got on.

Dixon broke into a frenzied, lung-igniting sprint, while the conductor watched him immobile from the platform. When he was halfway to the bus, this official rang the bell, the driver let in the clutch, and the wheels began to turn. Dixon found he was even better at running than he'd thought, but when the gap between man and bus had narrowed to perhaps five yards, it began to widen rapidly. Dixon stopped running and favoured the conductor, who was still watching unemotionally, with the best-known obscene gesture. At once the conductor rang the bell again and the bus stopped abruptly. Dixon hesitated for a moment, then trotted lightly up to the bus and boarded it with some diffidence. He found himself unwilling to meet the eye of the conductor, who now said admiringly 'Well run, wacker' and rang the bell for the third time.

"Lorry, trailer and bus began moving, at a steady twelve miles an hour, round what gave firm promise of being a long series of bends."

Dixon gasped out a question about the bus's time of arrival at the station, which was where it terminated its run, got a civil but evasive answer, spent a few moments beating down the stares of the nearby passengers, and climbed effortfully to the top deck. There he made his rebounding way to the front seat and collapsed into it without being able to afford the breath to groan. He began swallowing the thick burning substance that filled his mouth and throat, panted energetically for a time, and tremulously took out his packet of small cigarettes and his matches. After reading the joke on the back of the matchbox a few times and laughing at it, he lit a cigarette; this was the only action he could take for the moment. He looked out of the window; the road unfolded itself in front of him, and he couldn't help feeling some sort of exhilaration, especially at the brightness of the landscape under the sun. Beyond the lines of green-tiled semi-detached villas open fields were already appearing, and through some trees he could see a gleam of water.

Christine had said that she'd 'understand' if he failed to turn up to see her off. What did that mean? Did it mean that she 'understood' that his commitments with Margaret would have decided him not to come? Or had it some vaguely unwelcome overtone, implying that she'd 'understand' that the whole thing between them now appeared to him as a romantic mistake, Margaret or no Margaret? He couldn't allow Christine to escape him to-day; if she did he might not see her again at all. Not at all; that was a disagreeable phrase. Suddenly his face altered, seeming to become all nose and glasses; the bus had moved up behind a lorry slowly drawing along an elaborate trailer, which had a notice on it recommending caution and saying how many feet long it was. A smaller notice adduced further grounds for caution in the elliptic form: *Air brakes.* Lorry, trailer, and bus began moving, at a steady twelve miles an hour, round what gave firm promise of being a long series of bends. With difficulty Dixon snatched his gaze from the back of the trailer and, to fortify himself, began thinking about what Catchpole had said to him about Margaret.

He realised at once that his mind had been made up as soon as he decided to make this journey. For the first time he really felt that it was no use trying to save those who fundamentally would rather not be saved. To go on trying would not merely be to yield to pity and sentimentality, but wrong and, to pursue it to its conclusion, inhumane. It was all very bad luck on Margaret, and probably derived, as he'd thought before, from the anterior bad luck of being sexually unattractive. Christine's more normal, *i.e.* less unworkable, character no doubt resulted, in part at any rate, from having been lucky with her face and figure. But that was simply that. To write things down as luck wasn't the same as writing them off as non-existent or in some way beneath consideration. Christine was still nicer and prettier than Margaret, and all the deductions that could be drawn from that fact should be drawn: there was no end to the ways in which nice things are nicer than nasty ones. It had been luck, too, that had freed him from pity's adhesive plaster; if Catchpole had been a different sort of man, he, Dixon, would still be wrapped up as firmly as ever. And now he badly needed another dose of luck. If it came, he might yet prove to be of use to somebody.

"Was the driver slumped in his seat, the victim of syncope, or had he suddenly got an idea for a poem?"

The conductor now appeared and negotiated with Dixon about his ticket. When this was over, he said: 'One forty-three we're due at the station. I looked it up.'

'Oh. Shall we be on time, do you think?'

'Couldn't say. I'm sorry. Not if we keep crawling behind this Raf contraption we shan't, I shouldn't think. Train to catch?'

'Well, I want to see someone who's getting the one-fifty.'

'Shouldn't build on it if I were you.' He lingered, no doubt to examine Dixon's black eye.

'Thanks,' Dixon said dismissively.

They entered a long stretch of straight road, with a slight dip in the middle so that every yard of its empty surface was visible. Far ahead an emaciated brown hand appeared from the lorry's cab and made a writhing, beckoning movement. The driver of the bus ignored this invitation in favour of drawing to a gradual halt by a bus-stop outside a row of thatched cottages. The foreshortened bulks of two old women dressed in black waited until the bus was quenched of all motion before clutching each other and edging with sidelong caution out of Dixon's view towards the platform. In a moment he heard their voices crying unintelligibly to the conductor, then activity seemed to cease. At least five seconds passed; Dixon stirred elaborately at his post, then twisted himself about looking for anything that might have had a share in causing this caesura in his journey. He could detect nothing of this kind. Was the driver slumped in his seat, the victim of syncope, or had he suddenly got an idea for a poem? For a moment longer the pose prolonged itself; then the picture of sleepy rustic calm was modified by the fairly sudden emergence from a cottage some yards beyond of a third woman in a lilac costume. She looked keenly towards the bus and identified it without any obvious difficulty, then approached with a kind of bowed shuffle that suggested the movements of a service-man towards the pay-table. This image was considerably reinforced by her hat, which resembled a Guardsman's peaked cap that had been strenuously run over and then dyed cerise. Indeed, it was possible that the old bitch—a metallic noise came from the back of Dixon's throat when he saw her smile of self-admiration at having caught her bus—had actually found what was to become her hat lying in the road outside her nasty little cottage after a military exercise, the legacy of some skylarking lout in the carrier platoon, from whose head it had fallen under the tracks and wheels of an entire battalion.

"Dixon thought he really would have to run downstairs and knife the drivers of both vehicles."

The bus nosed its prudential way on to the crown of the road, and the gap between it and the lorry began to diminish. Dixon found that his whole being had become centred in the matter of the bus's progress; he couldn't be bothered any longer to wonder what Christine would say to him if he got there in time, nor what he'd do if he didn't. He just sat there on the dusty cushions, galvanised by the pitchings of the bus into the appearance of seismic laughter, sweating stealthily in the heat and the apprehension—thank God he hadn't been drinking—, stretching his face in a fresh direction at each overtaking car, each bend, each motiveless circumspection of the driver.

The bus was now resolutely secured again behind the trailer, which soon began to reduce speed even further. Before Dixon could cry out, before he'd time to guess what was to happen, the lorry and trailer had moved off to the side into a lay-by and the bus was travelling on alone. Now was the time, he thought with reviving hope, for the driver to start making up some of the time he must have lost. The driver, however, was clearly unable to assent to this diagnosis. Dixon lit another small cigarette, jabbing with the match at the sandpaper as if it were the driver's eye. He had, of course, no idea of the time, but estimated that they must, by now, have covered five of the eight or so miles to their destination. Just then the bus rounded a corner and slowed abruptly, then stopped.

"Before the bus had reached the station stop he plunged down, out, across the road and into the booking-hall."

Making a lot of noise, a farm tractor was laboriously pulling, at right angles across the road, something that looked like the springs of a giant's bed, caked in places with earth and decked with ribbon-like grasses. Dixon thought he really would have to run downstairs and knife the drivers of both vehicles; what next, what next? What actually would be next: a masked hold-up, a smash, floods, a burst tyre, an electric storm with falling trees and meteorites, a diversion, a low-level attack by Communist aircraft, sheep, the driver stung by a hornet? He'd choose the last of these, if consulted. Hawking its gears, the bus crept on, while every few yards troupes of old men waited to make their quivering way aboard.

As the traffic thickened slightly towards the town, the driver added to his hypertrophied caution a psychopathic devotion to the interests of other road-users; the sight of anything between a removal-van and a junior bicycle halved his speed to four miles an hour and sent his hand, Dixon guessed, flapping in a slow-motion St. Vitus' dance of beckonings and waving-on. Learners practised reversing across his path; gossiping knots of loungers parted leisurely at the touch of his reluctant bonnet; toddlers reeled to retrieve toys from under his just-revolving wheels. Dixon's head switched angrily to and fro in vain search for a clock; the inhabitants of this mental, moral and physical backwater, devoting as they had done for years their few waking moments to the pursuit of offences against chastity, were too poor, and were also too mean . . . Dixon, seeing the hulk of the railway station thirty yards off, returned painfully to reality and rattled along the aisle to the stairs. Before the bus had reached the station stop he plunged down, out, across the road and into the booking-hall. The clock over the ticket-office pointed to one forty-seven. At once the minute hand stepped one pace onward. Dixon flung himself at the barrier. A hard-faced man confronted him.

'Which platform for London, please?'

The man looked at him appraisingly, as if trying to gauge in advance his fitness to hear a more than usually improper joke. 'Bit early, aren't you?'

'Eh?'

'Next to London's eight-seventeen.'

'Eight-seventeen?'

'No restaurant car.'

'What about the one-fifty?'

'No one-fifty. Haven't got it mixed up with the one-forty, by any chance?'

Dixon swallowed. 'I think I must have done,' he said. 'Thanks.'

'Sorry, George.'

(From *Lucky Jim*)

The Saint takes a Bus

Leslie Charteris

Simon Templar was used to more exotic transport than the old Sicilian bus he was forced to use on this occasion. But Templar, the Saint, was being hunted by the Mafia, and there was no other choice if he wanted to survive.

Every run of bad cards must have a break, however brief, as every gambler knows; and as the Saint reached the main road at last, and his visualisation of the most imminent menace still had the warriors up the hill only now looking for a place to turn their oversize chariot, it seemed to him that his turn was veritably setting in. For less than a hundred yards away on his right, a heavily laden *autobus* was grinding noisily towards him, with the inspiring name PALERMO on the front to indicate its destination.

There were no other vehicles in sight at this moment, and no surly characters with artillery in their pockets to bar his way. The next steps towards escape only had to be taken across the highway, and called for no additional effort beyond flagging down the driver.

Brakes protested, and the bus lurched to a stop. Simon climbed in, the door slammed behind him, and he was on his way again.

But as he paid his fare, he felt that his arrival was causing a minor stir among the passengers. It was a local bus, and the riders seemed to consist mostly of regional habitants and their produce, progeny, and purchases. Perhaps that was the cause of their interest: the Saint was a stranger and obviously a different type, and for lack of anything better to do they would study and speculate about him. Yet there seemed to be an undercurrent of tension running counter to this simple bucolic curiosity. Unless he was excessively self-conscious, he felt as if the other passengers were allowing him far more room than they gave each other. In fact, he had a distinct impression that they were moving as far away from him as the packed conditions would allow.

Considering the aromas of garlic and honest sweat which pervaded the interior in multiple combinations with other less readily recognisable perfumes, it was somewhat disturbing to speculate on what exotic odour he might be diffusing about which even the best Sicilian wouldn't tell him. Perhaps he was being unduly sensitive; but the events of that day and the previous night would have undermined anyone's confidence in his popularity or social magnetism.

He tried his most innocent and endearing smile on one of the women nearest to him, who was staring into his face with a fixed intensity which suggested either extreme myopia or partial hypnosis, and she crossed herself hurriedly and squirmed back into the engulfing crowd with a look of startled panic.

He hadn't been imagining things. Someone had already identified him, and the whispered word had been passed around.

The fact could be read now in the tense lines of their bodies, their petrified immobility or nervous fidgeting, and the way their eyes fastened on him and then slid away when he looked in their direction. The Saint's description had clearly been circulated throughout the entire district, with promises of reward for finding and/or threats of punishment for hiding him, and in every crowd there was likely to be one who had heard it.

There didn't seem to be any Mafia hirelings on the bus itself, or they would already have gone into action; but he could expect no allies either. None of these people might actively try to attack him, nor would they give him any aid or comfort. Even if they were not sympathisers with the Mafia, they had been terrorised for so long that they would do exactly what the organisation had ordered.

The bus ground protestingly up the grades and clattered recklessly down the alternating slopes that made up for them, obedient to the latent death-wish of the normal Italian driver; and with each kilometre the suspense

At each stop there was a rearrangement of seating and standing room, until there were only men around him, uneasy but grim.

---

drew tauter, but not from the inherent uncertainties of Sicilian public transportation.

Sometimes the conveyance stopped to pick up new travellers or to let others off; and Simon did not need extrasensory perception to know that as soon as telephones could be reached the wires would be humming with reports of his sighting.

And at each stop there was a rearrangement of seating and standing room, until there were only men around him, uneasy but grim. He wondered how much longer it would be before one of them might be tempted to try for a medal, and he moved his hand to rest it near the butt of the gun under his shirt.

If the pressure seemed to be creeping too close to an explosion point he would have to get off before Palermo. It might be a wise precaution in any case. He had no idea how long the full trip would take, but it would certainly be long enough for a welcoming delegation to muster at the terminus. The equation of survival that had to be solved required a blind guess at the unknown length of time he could stay with the bus to gain the maximum escape mileage, before warnings telephoned ahead would have a reception committee assembled and waiting for him at the next stop.

He had been keeping most of his attention on the other riders, who had packed themselves closer to suffocation in their desire to keep beyond contamination range of him, but he had been careful to reserve some portion of his awareness for the outside world through which they travelled. He was not concerned with noting all the spots of scenic interest, but with observing any other vehicles whose occupants might evince unusual interest in the one he rode in. And now his circumspection suddenly paid off. A large American sedan pulled around from behind the bus with a screaming horn, as if to pass it, and then simply stayed level with it, while swarthy faces carefully scanned the interior.

Trying not to make any sharp conspicuous movement, Simon edged farther towards the opposite side, bending his knees and slumping his spine to diminish his height, and trying to keep the heads of other passengers between the parallel car and the smallest segment of his face which would let him keep an eye on it and its occupants.

It was a good try, but there was a typically neutralist consensus against it. As his fellow travellers also became aware of the car keeping alongside, they separated and shrank away, either as a pharisaic way of pointing him out without pointing, or to remove themselves from the line of fire if there was to be any shooting. Either way, the result was disastrously the same. A lane opened up across the bus, with passengers trampling each other's corns on both sides but leaving a clear space between Simon and the windows. Even the seated riders found themselves suddenly irked by the burden on their buttocks, and got up to join the sardine pack of standees.

Simon Templar, willy-nilly, was given as unobstructed a view of the men in the car as they were given of him.

But after the first glance there was only one face that held his attention: the face of the man in front, beside the driver. A fat, reddened, unshaven face that cracked in a lipless grin like a triumphant lizard as the recognition became mutual.

The face of Al Destamio.

Simon wished he had been wearing a hat, so that he could have raised it in a mocking salute that seemed to be the only possible gesture at the moment. Instead, he had to be content with giving his pursuer a radiant smile and a friendly wave which was not returned.

Destamio's exultant travesty of a grin was replaced by a vindictive snarl. The barrel of an automatic appeared over the sill of his open window, and he steadied it with both hands to aim.

The Saint's smile also faded as he snatched the pistol from his belt and ducked

"That stop has been discontinued" said the Saint, and his forefinger moved ever so slightly on the trigger. "Keep going."

to shelter as much of himself as posisble below the dubious steel of the bus's coachwork. He had no misgivings as to who would be the victor in a straight shoot-out under those conditions; but when Destamio's henchmen chimed in, as they would without caring how many bystanders were killed or injured in the exchange, a lot of non-combatants were likely to become monuments to another of the perils of neutralism. And pusillanimous as they might have shown themselves, and perhaps undeserving of too much consideration, Simon had to think of the consequences to himself of a lucky score on the bus driver at that speed.

The problem was providentially resolved when Destamio suddenly disappeared. His startled face slid backwards with comical abruptness, taking the car with it, as if it had been snagged by some giant hook in the pavement; it took Simon an instant to realise that it was because the driver had been forced to jam on his brakes and drop back to avoid a head-on collision with oncoming traffic. No sooner had the sedan swung in behind the bus than an immense double-trailered truck roared by in the opposite direction, followed by a long straggle of weaving honking cars that had accumulated behind it.

The Saint didn't wait to see any more. His guardian angel was apparently trying to outdo himself, but there was no guarantee of how long that inordinate effort would continue. He had to make the most of it while it lasted—and before a break in the eastbound lane gave the Mafia chauffeur a chance to draw level again.

Through the broad windshield could be seen the outskirts of a city, and a cogwheeled sign whipped by with its international invitation to visiting Rotarians, followed by the name CEFALU. Now he knew where he was, and it would do for another stage.

As he pushed towards the front again, and the door, one of the men in a seat behind the driver was leaning forward to mutter something in his ear, and the bus was slowing.

"There is no need to stop," Simon said clearly. "No one wants to get off yet."

He was in the right-hand front corner by then, one shoulder towards the windshield and the other towards the door, and the gun in his hand was for everyone to see but especially favoured the driver.

"I am supposed to stop here," the man mumbled, his foot wavering between the accelerator and the brake.

"That stop has just been discontinued," said the Saint, and his forefinger moved ever so slightly on the trigger. "Keep going."

The bus rumbled on, and its other passengers glowered at the Saint sullenly, no longer trying to avoid his gaze, plainly resenting the danger that he had brought to them more violently and immediately than if he had been the carrier of a plague, but not knowing what to do about it. Simon remained impersonally alert and let his gun do all the threatening. Everyone received the message and declined to argue with it; the driver stared fixedly ahead and gripped the wheel as if it had been a wriggling snake.

From behind came repeated blares from the horn of the following sedan, and fresh sweat beaded the driver's already moist forehead. Through the length of the bus and over the heads of the other riders, Simon could catch glimpses of the sedan hanging on their tail and fretting for a chance to draw alongside again, but the increasing traffic of the town gave it no opening. And in the longitudinal direction, the passengers who were now crowded into the rear two-thirds of the bus could not open up a channel through which the Saint could be fired at from astern. Yet with all its advantages, it was a situation which could only be temporary: very soon, a traffic light or a traffic cop or some other hazard must intervene to change it, or the pursuing *mafiosi* would become more desperate and start shooting at the tyres.

"Anyone who gets out in less than two minutes will probably be shot," he announced, and pulled the lever that controlled the door next to him.

Simon decided that it was better to keep the initiative while he had it. He threw a long glance at the road ahead, then turned to wave the passengers back into submission before any of them could capitalise on his momentary inattention.

"Put your foot over the brake," he told the driver, "but do not touch it until I tell you to. Then give it all your weight—which can be alive or dead, as you prefer."

He had photographed the next quarter-mile of road on his memory, and now he waited for the first landmark he had picked to go by.

"Hold on tight, *amici,*" he warned the passengers. "We are going to make a sudden stop, and I do not want you to fall on your noses—or on this very hard piece of metal."

Again, through a momentary opening in the crowd, he glimpsed the trailing sedan edging out behind the left rear corner. And the wine-shop sign he had chosen for a marker was just ahead of the driver. The timing was perfect.

"*Ora!*" he yelled, and braced himself.

The brakes bit, and the bus slowed shudderingly. The standing passengers stumbled and collided and cursed, but miraculously held on to various props and managed to avoid being hurled down upon him in a human avalanche. And from the rear came a muted crash and crumpling sound, accompanied by a slight secondary jolt, which was the best of all he had hoped for.

The bus had scarcely even come to a complete standstill when he reached across the driver and in a swift motion turned off the ignition and removed the key.

"Anyone who gets out in less than two minutes will probably be shot," he announced, and pulled the lever that controlled the door next to him.

Then he was out, and one glance towards the rear confirmed that the Mafia sedan was now most satisfactorily welded to the back of the bus which it had been over-ambitiously trying to pass. Its doors were still shut, and the men in it, even if not seriously injured, were apparently still trying to pick themselves off the floor or otherwise pull themselves together. The car itself might or might not be out of the chase for a considerable time, but the bus solidly blocked any vehicular access to the alley across the entrance of which it had parked itself with a symmetry which the Saint could not have improved on if he had been driving it himself.

He had put the pistol back in his waistband under his shirt during the last second before he stepped out of the bus, so that there was nothing to make him noticeable except the fact that he was walking briskly away from the scene of an interesting accident instead of hurrying towards it like any normal native. But even so, those who passed him were probably too busy hustling to secure a front-row position in the gathering throng to pay any attention to his eccentric behaviour.

(From *Vendetta for the Saint*)

The Bus in Cartoons

Brockbank

Bert Thomas

BUS DRIVER: "Wotcher stoppin' for, mate?"
MIDGET DRIVER: "I was just waiting for you to say something funny."

Hector Breeze

"Of course I was doing over sixty!"

Sempe

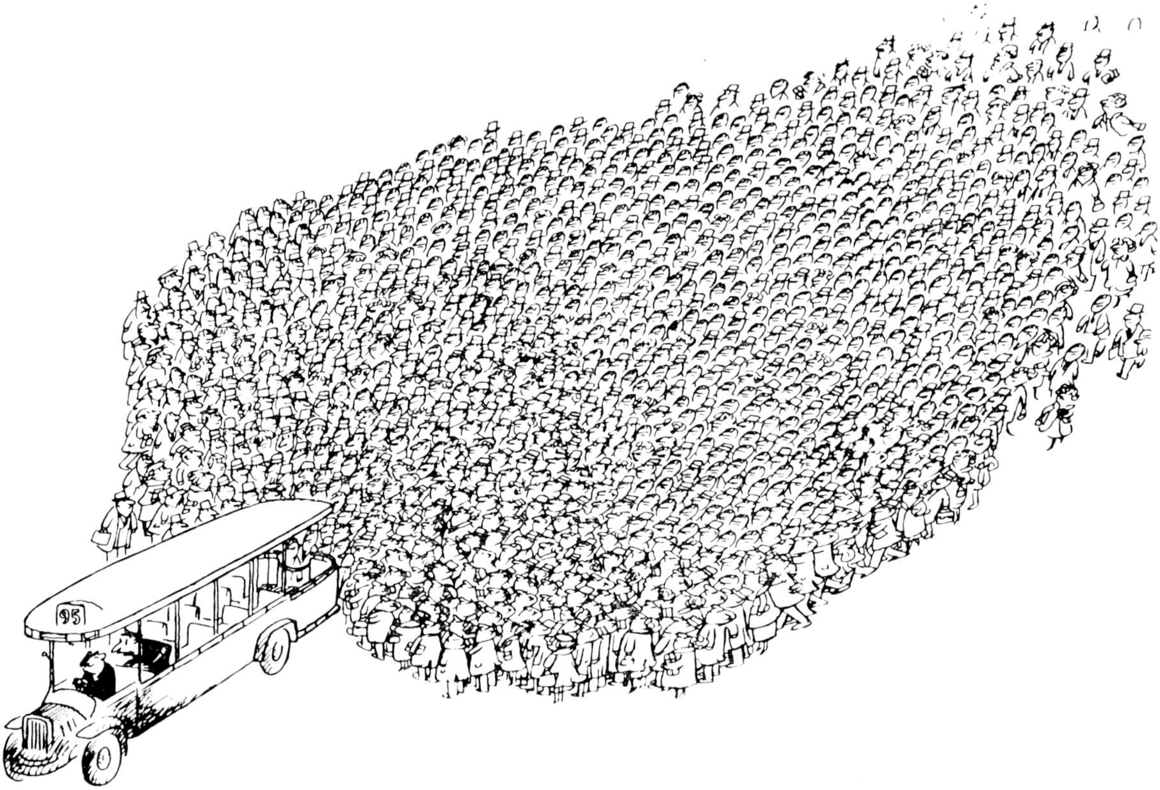

"*George, I'm frightened!*"

Ronald Searle

Giles

"That's only one hazard—her Ronnie ain't well enough to go to school so he has to come to work with her."

"Boy—with their regular bus on strike, are they glad to see me. Raise your 'at to 'em as we go by."

Brockbank

The bus in Films

The bus has never really achieved film stardom in the same way that cars ("Genevieve") and trains ("The Titfield Thunderbolt") have. These are a few that have won more than just drive-on parts.

ABOVE: A former Bournemouth Corporation Leyland Titan TD5 ends up in the sea at Teignmouth after a chase in "Press for Time"
RIGHT: The ex-Jersey Leyland Lion from the British Transport collection, disguised for its appearance as an Edinburgh bus in "The Prime of Miss Jean Brodie".
[Leyland: Gavin Booth

One recent film where a bus did play a big—almost a starring—part was Warner-Pathe's "Summer Holiday", released in 1963. In it Cliff Richard and company drove and sang across Europe in a couple of London Transport RTs. The distributors issued this hand-out at the time of release.

DESTINATION EUROPE!

Imagine just for a moment you're standing at a bus stop in London waiting as usual for your transport to the office.

A bus draws up and you go to get on . . . then you stop, rub your eyes and look again. For this bus is like no other you've ever seen!

For one thing, a pair of double doors are placed across the platform entrance. And, incredibly, the bus has curtains up at the windows! Through the windows you can see a range of kitchen equipment where the seats should be and hanging on the wall, a row of gleaming utensils—pots, pans, scoops, ladles and mixers.

All right—so you're never likely to see a bus like that. But you will if you go to see Cliff Richards' latest musical—the Elstree Distributors' Production "SUMMER HOLIDAY" for Warner-Pathe release.

For it is just such a bus that figures in this gay, song-laced story about a gang of London Transport mechanics and drivers who holiday across Europe in an old bus which they've done up for the occasion.

And there's no doubt about it—a good, solid bus makes an ideal holiday home.

Look what you've got—a lower deck for cooking and eating; an upper-deck for sleeping and toilet facilities. Plenty of room plus a bird's-eye view of the countryside tearing past.

No limit to numbers either—why, at one point in the film Cliff and his gang are invaded by a travelling troupe of entertainers led by Ron Moody and even then there's room to move!

For much of the journey, though, it's Cliff, co-star Lauri Peters and talented feature players such as Melvyn Hayes, Teddy Green, Jeremy Bulloch, Pamela Hart, Una Stubbs and Jackie Daryl who make up the bus's passenger list.

Originally it was only going to be Cliff and his male pals, but on their journey through France they meet up with three charming girls on their way to Athens and when their little car is wrecked, what can Cliff and the boys do but offer them a lift?

The distinctive red buses of London Transport became a familiar sight all across Europe and into Greece while "SUMMER HOLIDAY" was shooting its sun-splashed way through the summer of '62.

They (there were two, in case one broke down—but it never did!) rolled along Paris's Champs Elysee; through the dust-bowl of Yugoslavia and so into Greece, nosing round Constitution Square and on under the shadow of the towering Acropolis.

Afterwards, Cliff Richard said he wouldn't mind ever living in a converted bus for a holiday—it was so comfortable!

Other members of the cast echoed his view and the two studio drivers whose job it was to take the buses across Europe were full of praise for the way they tackled difficult terrain.

Said one: "They drive like a tank—you can never imagine them stopping or finding a gradient too tough to tackle."

So next time you board one of London's red buses—take another look at it. . . .

Because, let's face it, London's buses are something special now they've been the star (well, almost!) of a big CinemaScope and Eastmancolour film musical!

FACING PAGE: A scence from "Summer Holiday", with one of the RT 'stars'. [*Associated British*

What is this that roareth thus?

A. D. Godley

What is this that roareth thus?
Can it be a Motor Bus?
Yes, the smell and hideous hum
Indicat Motorem Bum!
Implet in the Corn and High
Terror me Motoris Bi:
Bo Motori clamitabo
Ne Motore caedar a Bo—
Dative be or Ablative
So thou only let us live:
Whither shall thy victims flee?
Spare us, spare us, Motor Be!
Thus I sang; and still anigh
Came in hordes Motores Bi,
Et complebat omne forum
Copia Motorum Borum.
How shall wretches live like us
Cincti Bis Motoribus?
Domine, defende nos
Contra hos Motores Bos!

The Village Bus that Nobody Missed

Barbara Ovstedal

Waiting for a country bus was always an event. Sometimes it meant popping a letter into the red postbox that hung on its side. At other times it was a trip into town with pocket-money to spend.

The bus in my life was the *Silver Queen*. She was silver-grey in colour and plied between the Sussex village of Slindon and the little seaside town of Bognor—long before the Regis was added on to it. That bus took me to school and to the seashore. I rode home on her to buttered crumpets in winter and to cool lemonade in summer. She dropped me off outside the church on Sundays. I remember her gay with flags on the day of the Silver Jubilee.

The *Silver Queen* was one of the early country buses. She was born, in the shape of a converted army ambulance, in Eastergate village one bright morning in 1919. Her owner, Cecil Walling, with his round, smiling face and battered trilby, was as much part of the country scene as the bus he drove. And his dialect was as pure and local as Sussex drip-pudding.

He knew everyone by name, pushing back the window to call, 'Hallo, Will !' or 'Morning Bert !' from the driver's seat as he passed by. The landlords of all the pubs en route had his time-tables hanging up in the bars and booked parties for outings to the Fontwell and Goodwood Races.

Yet that morning in 1919 when Cecil took his *Silver Queen* on to the road for the first time it seemed as if nobody wanted to ride in her. He had pasted up his newly-printed timetables, and had paid 17s. 6d. for a hackney carriage licence. The tank was filled up with commercial petrol at 8d. per gallon, and he was ready for his first fares. But nobody hailed. People just stood and stared as he drove by. The whole route was covered twice without picking up a single passenger.

Then Cecil overtook two country women trudging along with baskets on their arms. He stopped, jumped out, and swung open the door in the back of the bus.

"Step in, ladies," he invited. 'No need to walk four miles into town today.'

The Silver Queen, a normal-control Daimler, PX143, that worked between Slindon and Bognor in the early 1920s.

They hesitated, looking longingly at the bus.

'What's the fare?' one asked.

'It's expensive to ride in them things, isn't it?' asked the other.

'You are my first passengers,' Cecil answered. 'You shall ride free today.' They climbed in excitedly and settled themselves down on the wooden seats. Cecil drove into town as proud as a peacock.

Cecil loved to tell his story of his first day on the road. He often told while delaying the bus's departure for a regular passenger who had not yet arrived. I would sit in the front of the bus, the shiny black leather seat made hot by the sun and burning the back of my bare legs. The bus always had a warm and comfortable smell of petrol and old boots and summer hay. 'We never leave anyone behind,' Cecil used to boast, taking his gold watch out of his waistcoat pocket to see how many minutes he would have to make up that time.

People never minded sitting in the bus and waiting for a latecomer. After all, the next time it might be their turn to be late, and it was nice to know that the bus would always wait for you. But there was a time when a passenger named Mr. Ossie, an elderly stockbroker, was almost left behind.

The *Silver Queen* had made a special trip to the Goodwood Races. A local publican, Ernie Hunt, was filling in as conductor. At the end of the afternoon everyone got back into the bus, and it was one of the first to drive out of the charabanc park on the journey home. Half a mile down the road the conductor discovered that Mr. Ossie was missing. The brakes slammed. The bus stopped with a jerk. Cecil sent Ernie Hunt running back to find the missing passenger.

Then Cecil jumped out, lifted the bonnet, and started tinkering with the engine—not an uncommon sight in those early days of motoring. A few moments later a mounted policeman came riding up, for the Metropolitan police always came down to control the traffic in race week.

"You can't stop here!" roared the police sergeant. 'Move on! You're holding up everybody!' Cecil looked up, his expression innocent. 'She won't budge,' he said. 'Can't get her started.' (Of course not—with the engine switched off!)

The sergeant roared and spluttered, wheeling his horse round to face the gathering queue of hooting motor cars. In the narrow lane the bus was taking up so much room that no vehicle could pass.

Just then Ernie Hunt came belting back down the road. Mr. Ossie followed behind, holding on to his topper with a cream-gloved hand, his coat-tails flying. The two men leapt on to the bus. Cecil threw himself into the driver's seat. The bus charged off with speed that sent everyone shooting backwards in their seats. In the mirror Cecil saw the police sergeant shaking his fist after the bus. He gave a satisfied chuckle. The tradition of the *Silver Queen* had not been broken.

I grew up hopping on and off that bus. Sometimes I helped the conductor by running up a path with a packet of fish for somebody's tea. At other times I watched Cecil collect a parcel to be posted, a watch that needed mending, or even a book to be changed at the library. Nothing was too much trouble for the crew of the *Silver Queen*.

As time went by bigger companies tried to squeeze this little bus service off the road. Conductors of rival buses would sometimes shout out to a waiting queue that the *Silver Queen* had broken down. "That's all right," some local voice would reply. "We'll wait just the same, thankee."

Then the scene changed. There were soldiers on the bus and airmen from Tangmere. Canadians sat on the roof when the bus was full at night, singing as Cecil drove through the blacked-out countryside with the aid of two tiny points of light. Cecil and his conductor patched up the windows with cardboard and brown paper when blast from bombs shattered them. And they pointed out the holes in the roof where a Messerschmitt had machine-gunned them.

I came home for Christmas in 1944 and rode on the *Silver Queen* for the last time. Cecil had decided to retire. The route that he had travelled for many years was swallowed up by larger bus companies.

(From *Country Life*)

From one who got away

Clement Freud

When the passengers on Friday's 10 a.m. West End tour by London Transport reassembled in the coach, after alighting at Buckingham Palace to observe the Changing of the Guard, one was missing. A man in a grey suit with a notebook and pencil.

I should like to apologise to the two elderly Flemish ladies, to the couple from Leamington with their bucktooth daughter and the five Americans who appeared to have been subjected to the ministrations of a totalitarian hairdresser; regrets also to the strong, silent Bavarian and his spouse, and to the three gentlemen from Pakistan, for any inconvenience caused. I was the missing man—I jumped into a passing taxi and got away. I had had enough.

It started at Victoria coach station. A disorderly queue for tickets marshalled by a man of small charm wearing a hat called LCC Ltd. The two Cs stood for Coastal Coaches. The West End tour cost 12s. 6d.; bay 2 or 3 they said. I examined the bays in question and found buses offering the uncompulsive choice of Leicester or Manchester. Inquiries suggested that West End might come up behind Manchester at 9.50; it did.

We left Victoria at ten past ten. By this time the driver had been in and out of his seat three or four times and the guide had counted us twice, compared us with his list of reservations, clucked and informed us that we were four short. As there was little we could do about the deficiency we just looked suitably guilty, and he said never mind, we'll go now. We went. He took off his cap, tapped a microphone for some moments and then started to talk.

Good morning folks, he said. We are going now on a tour of the principal thoroughfares of the West End of London including a visit to Buckenham Palace. Sit back and relax.

There was little chance to do either: within three minutes he had asked us to look at the Royal Society of Health (he pronounced it Helf), Victoria Station—serving 16 places on the South Coast and Gatwick Airport with daily flights to the Continent and Africa—the Lifeboat Society who save thousands of lives, the offices of the Coal Board and Godfrey Winn's house. He had missed two fire engines and 12 firemen rushing up a building opposite the Grosvenor Hotel. Can you hear me at the back, he shouted as we approached Hyde Park Corner; unable to deny this we nodded miserably.

A hundred and twenty-one thousand vehicles pass here daily between 8 a.m. and 8 p.m.—don't let the dust-cart get in the way driver—and don't worry about the Quadrega, I'll explain that later he shouted at us. Off we went down the East Carriage Drive: on your right the statue of Lord Byron, the Greek national hero and over there the Royal Hilton Hotel.

Soon we were in Oxford Street. He had not drawn a noticeable breath since we left Buckingham Palace Road. "Oxford Street, the ladies' paradise—don't worry gentlemen we're not stopping—and there is the store of Gordon Selfridge, a very imposing entrance I think you will agree."

Selfridge, he said, started in a small way, created this and when he died he died propertyless. Some of the interior is by Holbrook Jackson—he done the clock—and other ornamentations is by Reid Dick. We moved past the Cumberland into the Bayswater Road. Now this, he said, is where we are in Hyde Park—the large building there is the Royal Hilton what we passed.

In an ensuing nightmare of facts and figures we passed a crematorium for animals which we just missed because the driver took the bend too fast, saw the Elbert Memorial, the Victoria and Elbert Museum—you could spend a week there—and onto the Brompton Road: "many antique shops here all owned by tip-top people." You can pur-chase many useful articles.

We passed a group of "statury" sculptured by Sir Jacob Epstein, the Ritz, Piccadilly

(continued on next page

Drivers Wild/2

Red Daniells

I've not been on this one but a month or two. It's one of the new high-speed lots designed for the M1 and similar. I've just brought the local team down to play Squeamish United. Slagthorpe? Near Manchester—took us just over three hours. Aye, well, that's the beauty of it. This one's a goer, I can tell you. It's about time we had a turn at who gets first crack at the road. I got fed up going on the grass to let some flash lot and his fancy bird get by. I make 'em work for it now. I've had a few on to traffic islands, I'll tell you. They lose heart trying it on with this lot at eighty miles an hour. Besides, you have to go a bit to keep the average up, what with beer-stops and that. When we get supporters' clubs on board they all hang over the back of my seat geeing me up with rattles and blowing trumpets and you sort of gets into the spirit of the thing. Especially if our lot won. It's a right pantomime on the way home. Road courtesy? Nice hobby for them that's got the time to waste, but if you ask me it went out with the horse-trams. Today it's get on or get out. I'm after having a go at old Basher Clagg's record for the London-Manchester, but I think I'll wait till he comes out of hospital—if he ever does. [*From 'More Wild Drivers'*

Circus, "the hub of the world" with Eros the God of Love commemorating the Earl of Shaftesbury—a great philanderopist"—to Trafalgar Square, Parliament Square and back past Nelson into the Mall. As coaches are not normally permitted within the Royal Parks we were stopped by an official; unfortunately the driver produced a pass and we were let through. By the side of Buckingham Palace we stopped and our guide suggested that we get out. "Stick close together and I'll explain the Changing of the Guard." It was just then that I saw the taxi. . . .

As I said, I'm sorry, but I'm pretty sure the guide explained it all away. On future tours he might even point to the spot and say "It was here that we lost a man with a notebook in a grey suit on a rainy Friday morning in June."

(From *The Sunday Telegraph,*
June 30, 1963)

In Quotation Marks / 3

"Now is the time to make a plea for the comfort of the future motor bus driver in the winter. Anyone who has driven a car in the winter knows the discomfort—in fact we might say pain—of the performance. Few, however, can realise what it means to be out the length of the winter day with a steering wheel in one's hand."

[Motor Traction ; 1907

The photo shows an early SMT Maudslay, S550, of 1906 vintage. *[Scottish Omnibuses*

"The first hour or so's the worst. After you've gone numb from the knees down, you sort of settle in . . . Rain'll freeze on your face, and when you're really cold, you mustn't nod off for a nap in a lay-by."

[Bus chassis driver in "The Sunday Times"

The photo shows a driver delivering an Edinburgh Corporation Leyland PD3 chassis.

[R.L. Iles

And a final word....

EVERY INTENDING PASSENGERS ESSENTIAL GUIDE TO TRAVELLING BY OMNIBUS

Uncouthness Must Be Curbed

Refrain from Affectation

Keep your feet off the seats.

Do not get into a snug corner yourself and then open the window to admit a *north-westerly gale* down the neck of your neighbour.

Have your money ready. If *your* time is not valuable, that of others may be.

Do not impose upon the conductor the necessity of finding you change. He is not a banker.

Sit with your limbs straight, and do not let your legs describe an angle of forty-five degrees, thereby occupying the room of *two* passengers.

Do not spit upon the straw. You are not in a pig-sty, but in an omnibus, travelling in a country which boasts of its refinement.

Confined by a String

Behave respectfully to females, and put not an unprotected lass to the blush because she cannot escape from your brutality.

If you do bring a dog, let him be small and confined by a string.

Do not introduce large parcels. An omnibus is not a van.

Reserve bickerings and disputes for the open field. The sound of your own voice may be music in your own ears—not so, perhaps, to those of your companions.

If you will broach politics or religion, speak with moderation: all have a right to *their* opinions, and all have the right not to have them wantonly shocked.

Refrain from affectation and conceited airs. Remember you are riding for sixpence a distance which, if made in a hackney-coach would cost you *as many shillings*; and that, should your pride elevate you above plebeian accommodation, your purse should enable you to command aristocratic indulgence.

(From *The Times*, January 1836)

Acknowledgements

I am grateful to a number of people who gave me willing help when I was compiling this book. In addition to those listed below, I must mention my gratitude to my wife, who smilingly put up with several rooms ankle-deep in books, magazines, manuscripts and photographs, and with my general preoccupation with the job of compiling this book.

For permission to reproduce extracts from newspapers, magazines and books, I am indebted to the following:

'The Sunday Times' for the extracts from *The Next Transport Age* by George Perry and for *Lord Egremont and the Phantom Motorbus* by Atticus.

Leyland Motors Ltd for the extract from *Seventy Years of Progress.*

Tony Hogg and the National Magazine Co Ltd for *Busman's Holiday* by Tony Hogg.

The Omnibus Society for *By Any Other Name* by J. E. Dunabin and *The Change* by H. Webb.

'Old Motor' for *Day Out* by K. C. Blacker.

The 'Leyland Journal' for *Seeing Niagara—From a London Bus.*

Scorpion Press for extracts from *Drivers Wild* and *More Wild Drivers* by Red Daniells.

The National Magazine Co Ltd for *Rugs, Straw and Decency: Take an Omnibus* by Jan Condel.

'Design' magazine for extracts from *Pioneering Policies* by Corin Hughes-Stanton.

London Transport for extracts from *London Transport Posters.*

Michael Flanders for *A Transport of Delight* by Michael Flanders and Donald Swann.

Victor Gollancz Ltd for the extract from *Lucky Jim* by Kingsley Amis.

Hodder & Stoughton Ltd for the extract from *Vendetta for the Saint* by Leslie Charteris.

Oxford University Press for *What is it that Roareth Thus*? by A. D. Godley, from *50 Poems of A. D. Godley*.

Barbara Ovstedal and 'Country Life' for *The Village Bus that Nobody Missed* by Barbara Ovstedal.

Clement Freud and the 'Sunday Telegraph' for *From One Who Got Away* by Clement Freud.

The cartoons and drawings are reproduced by courtesty of the following:

Mrs. Josephine Heath Robinson for *History Repeats Itself* by Heath Robinson, from *Absurdities.*

Russell Brockbank for the two Brockbank cartoons.

'Punch' for the Bert Thomas cartoon.

'Private Eye' for the Hector Breeze cartoon.

Sempe and Christiane Charillon for the Sempe cartoon.

Ronald Searle and Hope, Leresche & Steele for the Ronald Searle cartoon.

Giles and the 'Daily Express' for the two Giles cartoons.

I am particularly grateful to those gentlemen who responded to my appeals for original contributions, namely J. M. Aldridge, Chas. S. Dunbar, James FitzJames, R. N. Hannay, P. J. Marshall, John F. Parke, K. W. Swallow and A. Alan Townsin.

Background to the Bus Industry by R. L. Iles is an updated version of an article that appeared in 'Buses Illustrated' for February 1967.

Old Booth's Almanack is based on two articles of the same name I contributed to the 'Omnibus Magazine' for December 1965 and December 1966.

The following individuals and firms kindly supplied photographs: AEC Ltd, Albion Motors Ltd, Arlington Motor Co, Associated British Productions Ltd, M. J. Banfield, D. G. Bowen, J. F. Burns, G. T. Coxon, R. T. Coxon, A. B. Cross, J. E. Dunabin, Duple Group Sales, Ford of Britain, R. L. Grieves, R. L. Iles, Jaguar Cars Ltd, Leyland Motors Ltd, London Transport Board, P. J. Marshall, T. W. Moore, A. Moyes, J. H. Napier, Old Motor, Meccano Ltd, Mettoy Co Ltd, National Benzole, Charles H. Roe Ltd, Scottish Omnibuses Ltd, Seddon Motors Ltd, C. T. Shears, R. H. G. Simpson, K. W. Swallow, Travel Press & Publicity Co Ltd, Vauxhall Motors Ltd. Half-tone and four-colour blocks were kindly loaned by Jaguar Cars Ltd, The Leyland Journal, The Omnibus Magazine, The Scottish Omnibus, Transport Holding Company, Travel Press & Publicity Co Ltd.